D1505203

POUR ONE OUT

CHRIS VOLA

MORROW
GIFT

POUR ONE OUT

cocktail odes to TV's most dearly departed

For Luis

CONTENTS

INTRODUCTION

From frosted-tipped boy bands and Y2K paranoia to cargo pants and Napster, 1999 was a largely unremarkable (and often cringe-worthy) time, pop culturally speaking. But the impact of that year's best new television program—an HBO crime series about a diabolical-yet-alluring New Jersey wise guy named Tony—was anything but trite. *The Sopranos* took prime-time drama to previously unimagined heights, convincing serious actors and directors that a move to the small screen was no longer career suicide but rather a path to greater notoriety and acclaim. Along with the proliferation of DVDs, digital recording devices, and the streaming services that would go on to replace them, the show helped usher in a new era, in which TV has become a greater, more accessible part of the cultural consciousness than ever before.

Twenty years into this golden age of seemingly unlimited content, for millions of fans, our favorite TV characters are still much more than just (mostly) sexy faces beaming back at us in all their high-definition glory. Their motives, misdeeds, romances, and physical peculiarities are fodder for countless happy-hour diatribes, preposterous theory videos and podcasts, and savagely hilarious memes. When one of them dies, we might cheer, we might cry, we might bludgeon our viewing devices with replica swords and go on epic Twitter rants... but we always feel something.

The way I see it, there are only two options: You can live in a constant state of anxiety, dreading—or praying for—another epic fatality every time you fire up your Roku or Fire TV Stick. Or you can celebrate the unfortunate fictional souls who populate the TV universe in style, and numb your weeks (sometimes years) of accumulated emotions at the same time. How? you ask. With classic cocktails, of course!

Because 1999 wasn't just about award-winning mob operas. It was also around that time that a group of New York spirits professionals—like the Rainbow Room's Dale DeGroff, Milk & Honey's Sasha Petraske, and Pegu Club's Audrey Saunders—frustrated by a drinking landscape dominated by artificially sweetened, neon monstrosities, vodka sodas, and bland Cosmopolitans (sorry, Carrie Bradshaw!), began opening bars focused on long-forgotten drinks and fresh ingredients. Soon, a cocktail renaissance was in full swing, with suspender-clad bartenders around the world serving up their favorite well-crafted Prohibition-era and pre-Prohibition-era potations and putting their own unique spins on them, leading to an entire new library of "modern classics." Nowadays you'd be hard-pressed to find any self-professed booze connoisseur who hasn't at least attempted—with wildly varying degrees of success—an old-fashioned or daiquiri in the relative safety of their own kitchen or living room.

Pour One Out: Cocktail Odes to TV's Most Dearly Departed is a seamless marriage (i.e., the non-Hollywood variety) of two of today's most popular pastimes. It's an ideal tool for aspiring drink slingers and screen junkies looking to concoct the perfectly tailored toast for their favorite doomed heroes, deliciously despicable villains, tragic heartthrobs, fascinating historical failures, noxious neighbors, and fatally fuzzy friends, with mouthwatering recipes from both revered drinks manuals and some of the most innovative mixologists working today, cocktails whose names, flavors, and/or histories best embody the fictionally departed.

So the next time someone suggests a deep dive down a binge-worthy rabbit hole, make sure the Wi-Fi's connected and the liquor cabinet's stocked. The safety of even the most beloved characters is never guaranteed, and this way you'll be able to give them a proper send-off in the classiest (and most delicious) way possible should tragedy strike!

POUR ONE OUT

THE WIRE

"Omar comin'!"

Did two words ever strike more terror into the hearts of Baltimore's criminals? Not while the city's most notorious stick-up man haunted its streets. RIP, Omar Little.

Known for his shotgun-concealing trench coat and legendary whistle, Omar made his living by strategically robbing and brutalizing drug dealers. But this professional killer also had a strict moral code, showing nothing but tenderness to those he loved—and vengeance to those who might harm them.

When Brandon—Omar's boyfriend and associate thief—was horrifically tortured and murdered by drug lord Avon Barksdale's crew, Omar launched a years-long war that landed Barksdale in prison and most of his soldiers six feet under. Omar *tried* to retire to Puerto Rico, but was forced back to Baltimore to avenge his beloved mentor, Butchie, after Marlo Stanfield—Barksdale's successor—killed him. Abandoning all caution, our Robin Hood of the streets went on one last rampage before being shot by a low-level corner boy he might have noticed had he not been so consumed by his desire for retribution.

Despite his emotional downfall, Omar was still a one-man firing squad, who, at the top of his game, seemed more like an invincible apparition than a flesh-and-blood vigilante. The Mexican Firing Squad, first described in Charles H. Baker's *The Gentleman's Companion,* and named for that country's (and Omar's) preferred method of execution, is an equally formidable drink. Refreshingly tart, with a bloodred blend of tequila, citrus, and bitters, this concoction has more than enough depth to celebrate all the facets of a seriously complex man. An ideal nerve tonic for those who still get shivers when someone starts whistling "A-Hunting We Will Go."

OMAR LITTLE

mexican firing squad

2 ounces reposado tequila

3/4 ounce fresh lime juice

3/4 ounce pomegranate syrup (see page 201)

4 dashes of Angostura bitters

Club soda

1 lime wedge, for garnish

Combine the tequila, lime juice, pomegranate syrup, and bitters in a shaker. Whip (shake without ice) and pour into a long glass filled with ice (preferably one long ice cube, known as a Collins spear). Top with club soda. Garnish with the lime wedge.

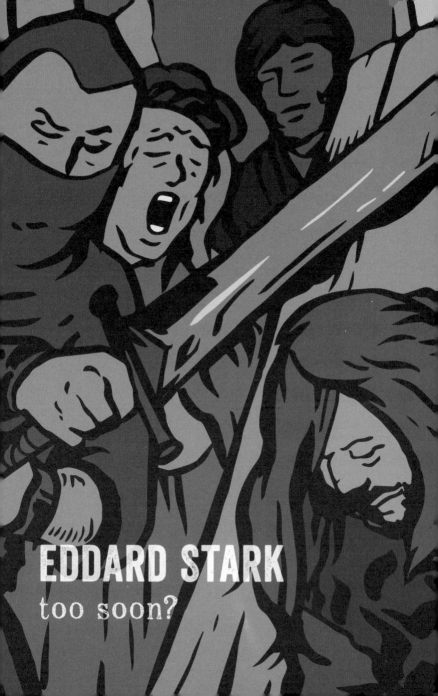

GAME OF THRONES

If being the fan-favorite protagonist of a wildly popular epic fantasy show came with a set of mandatory qualifications, dearly departed Lord Eddard "Ned" Stark checked all the boxes. Head of an ancient family and respected by the common folk? Check. Owner (and swinger) of a magically forged execution sword? Check. Ruggedly noble good looks *and* the gravitas to back them up? Double check. Ned spent his early years slaying the enemies of his king and best friend, Robert Baratheon, and later dutifully raising a handful of extraordinary (and occasionally murderous) children. When Robert asked Ned to move to King's Landing to become his Hand, Lord Stark seemed like the perfect choice to defend the crown and bring justice to Westeros's notoriously corrupt capital.

Nope. Ned's honorable nature held little sway in an urban cesspool of professional liars and schemers. In short, Ned failed: he failed at preventing Robert from being murdered; he failed at making Robert's wife, Cersei, pay for her incestuous crimes; and he failed at not being betrayed, imprisoned, and eventually beheaded at the request of Robert's illegitimate heir, Joffrey. After a mere nine episodes. This ultra-shocking demise gave rise to an unprecedented display of internet outrage, with thousands of fans swearing off *Game of Thrones* for good; a promise that has been broken as early and often as a Night's Watchman's vow of celibacy.

While the name of Sam Ross's Too Soon? cocktail ends in a question mark, there is no debate as to the untimeliness of Ned's death. This refreshing and savory gin sour variation features bright citrus notes with a subtle bitterness that lingers—much like the image of Ned's head stuck to a spike—long after the last sip. It's advisable to keep this easy-drinking recipe handy during any serious *Thrones* bingewatch, because as the show's devotees know all too well, Ned was only the first in an increasingly long line of beloved characters to fall prey to George R.R. Martin's twisted mind.

EDDARD STARK
too soon?

1 ounce gin
1 ounce Cynar or comparable
  artichoke liqueur
3/4 ounce fresh lemon juice

1/2 ounce simple syrup
  (see page 200)
2 thin slices orange

Combine the gin, Cynar, lemon juice, simple syrup, and 1 orange slice in an ice-filled shaker. Shake vigorously and strain into a stemmed cocktail glass. Garnish with the second orange slice.

SEINFELD

The most notable victim of self-described short, stocky, slow-witted bald man George Costanza, Susan Ross was destined for a sticky end. The NBC executive-within-a-show started dating George after he and Jerry Seinfeld pitched their ill-fated sitcom pilot to the network, a coupling that went down in flames. Literally. First Susan's parents' cabin burned down, exposing her father's secret romance with John Cheever, and then Susan herself was fired after George kissed her in front of her bosses.

After ending the relationship, Susan spent a brief period dating women. When George found out that her lesbianism "didn't take," he convinced her to marry him on a whim—and immediately regretted it. For the next year, he attempted to weasel out of the engagement by any means necessary—including trying to initiate an affair with a surprisingly receptive Marisa Tomei—but to no avail. He finally got his wish when Susan died after licking toxic glue on the envelopes he'd insisted on buying for their wedding invites.

The Airmail, first described in *Esquire*'s 1949 edition of *Handbook for Hosts*, thankfully tastes nothing like stationery adhesive. Its sweet, airy flavor reflects the tranquility, domestic or otherwise, that George briefly imagined he wanted; and its Champagne float hints at the luxurious lifestyle George would have enjoyed had Susan lived and inherited her Costanza-hating parents' considerable wealth. A popular signature drink at wedding receptions, the Airmail is a reminder that no part of one's nuptials, from the invitations to the cocktail hour, should ever be done on the cheap.

SUSAN ROSS

airmail

1 ounce light rum
1/2 ounce fresh lime juice

1/2 ounce honey syrup
  (see page 199)
1 ounce Champagne, chilled

Combine the rum, lime juice, and honey syrup in an ice-filled shaker. Shake vigorously and strain into a stemmed cocktail glass. Top with the Champagne.

WILD BILL HICKOK
gold rush

DEADWOOD

Of the thousands of hopeful gold-seekers who descended on Deadwood, South Dakota, in the 1870s, none was more notorious than James Butler "Wild Bill" Hickok. The famed gunslinger, former federal marshal, and professional gambler arrived at the unruly mining camp and quickly made a name for himself, rescuing a girl whose family had been massacred by road agents and earning the respect of the townsfolk with his deadly shooting abilities.

But above all else, Wild Bill was a poker fiend. His round-the-clock whiskey-fueled card binges provided him a steady income and were popular events at the saloons where he played—with no shortage of newly rich miners looking to get in on the action. Not everyone left the games impressed with Bill's cold, often condescending demeanor, though. One night, after losing several hands and being repeatedly insulted by Bill, a young drunkard named Jack McCall decided he'd had enough. The next day, McCall walked into Tom Nuttall's #10 Saloon, where Bill was playing another game—with his back uncharacteristically to the door—and fatally shot Deadwood's biggest celebrity in the back of the head.

The persistent threat of an untimely death, whether in a gold mine or at the poker table, did little to stem the tide of eighteenth-century prospectors rushing to the frontier. The Gold Rush, created by T. J. Siegel at New York's Milk & Honey in the early 2000s, is a masterfully revamped version of a traditional whiskey sour. Forgoing an egg white and substituting honey for simple syrup, the drink's smooth richness and golden hue evoke not only the seemingly endless natural bounty of the Old West but also Wild Bill's impressively flowing blond locks. A much tastier—and safer—poker game companion than a sidearm and a shot of rotgut.

WILD BILL HICKOK
gold rush

2 ounces bourbon
3/4 ounce fresh lemon juice

3/4 ounce honey syrup
(see page 199)

Combine the bourbon, lemon juice, and honey syrup in an ice-filled shaker. Shake vigorously and strain into a double old-fashioned glass over ice.

PARKS AND RECREATION

Pawnee, Indiana's most beloved celebrity was also its shortest. Lil' Sebastian, a miniature horse (*not* a pony), first delighted audiences at the 1987 Pawnee Harvest Festival, and was the eighth most photographed object in America that year. Leslie Knope, deputy director of the Pawnee Parks and Recreation Department, brought him out of retirement for the 2011 festival, where he again brought joy to all who gazed upon him (except Leslie's secret lover, Ben Wyatt, who didn't-and-still-doesn't see what all the fuss was about).

Sadly, not even legendary animals are immune to the ravages of time. Suffering from cataracts, arthritis, and diabetes (he and Parks Department scapegoat Jerry Gergich were "Glucotrol buddies"), Lil' Sebastian passed away soon after his final public appearance. News of his death sent shockwaves through Pawnee, culminating in a well-attended memorial service that featured a rousing performance of "5,000 Candles in the Wind," City Hall shoe-shiner and aspiring musician Andy Dwyer's epic tribute to the magically tiny beast, who, according to his obituary, was now "looking down on us, doing your two favorite things: eating carrots and urinating freely."

Though low in stature, Lil' Sebastian had an uncanny knack for raising the spirits of admirers of all ages. The

High Horse, introduced by Bobby Hicks at Manhattan's Lantern's Keep, is a modern classic that has quickly developed its own sizeable fan base. A surprisingly well-balanced fusion of citrusy, sweet, bitter, and smoky notes, the drink has something to appease almost every palate, a near universal appeal reminiscent of Pawnee's favorite equine. And while Parks Department director Ron Swanson suggested immortalizing Lil' Sebastian with a display rivaling the Super Bowl halftime show, the High Horse makes for a much tastier—and cost-effective—alternative.

LIL' SEBASTIAN
high horse

1 ounce reposado tequila
1 ounce Aperol
1 ounce fresh lime juice

1/2 ounce pomegranate syrup
  (see page 201)
1/4 ounce mezcal
1 lime wedge, for garnish

Combine the tequila, Aperol, lime juice, and pomegranate syrup in an ice-filled shaker. Shake vigorously and strain into a double old-fashioned glass over ice. Top with the mezcal. Garnish with the lime wedge.

ENOCH
THOMPSON
scofflaw

BOARDWALK EMPIRE

"I was happy," Enoch "Nucky" Thompson reminisced about his pre-Prohibition gig as a corrupt Atlantic City official. "Plenty of money, plenty of friends, plenty of everything. Then suddenly, plenty wasn't enough." Starting in 1919, the stylish and uncompromising city treasurer built a massive bootlegging empire and became one of the wealthiest men in America, while leaving an increasingly bloody trail of collateral damage that included troubled vet Jimmy Darmody, whom Nucky had helped raise and would ultimately kill. "You can't be half a gangster," Jimmy warned his mentor before being murdered by him in season 2.

Despite a spirit-crushing breakup with his wife, several brushes with death, and constant heat from federal investigators, Nucky continued to grow his empire for more than a decade, expanding his business down to Florida, where he hoped to retire with his girlfriend, Sally Wheet. But in 1931, with the repeal of Prohibition on the horizon, Nucky's luck suddenly ran dry. As undercover IRS agents closed in, Nucky was shot by none other than Tommy Darmody, son of Jimmy—a violent end for a man who had long profited from violence.

As much as Nucky strove to legitimize his businesses and mend broken relationships in his later years, it was his inescapable identity as an uncompromising crime boss that consumed—and ultimately doomed—the de facto King of Atlantic City.

A 1920s staple at Harry's Bar in Paris, the Scofflaw is a nod to those cutthroat industrialists who eased the suffering of millions of booze lovers during Prohibition—and grew immensely rich from it. This well-balanced blend of whiskey, vermouth, lemon juice, and grenadine has a citrusy-smooth flavor as crisp as Nucky's suit game, with a finish that's warm enough to remind even the most hardened lawbreaker of happier, simpler times.

ENOCH THOMPSON

scofflaw

1 ounce rye whiskey
1 ounce dry vermouth
3/4 ounce pomegranate syrup
 (see page 201)

1/2 ounce fresh lemon juice
2 dashes of orange bitters

Combine the rye, vermouth, pomegranate syrup, lemon juice, and bitters in an ice-filled shaker. Shake vigorously and strain into a stemmed cocktail glass.

PABLO ESCOBAR
blue collar

NARCOS

Many of history's notorious bad boys had humble beginnings, and Don Pablo was no exception. Rising from the turbulent streets of Colombia, Pablo Escobar went on to control 80 percent of the global cocaine market as the ruthless patron of the Medellín Cartel. Backed by his ludicrous wealth (think herd-of-pet-hippos rich) and his clout as a local philanthropist, he embarked on a presidential campaign to solidify his place among his country's greatest heroes.

But Colombia's political elite and Ronald Reagan weren't having it. Publicly outed as a drug lord, Pablo lost his congressional seat and ordered a slew of bombings and assassinations that left thousands dead and landed the Escobar family in prison, facing extradition. He narrowly escaped with his own life, and could only watch as his empire crumbled under the combined efforts of the DEA, CIA, and Colombian military. Desperate, broke, and cut off from his wife and children, he returned to Medellín, where, after a brief manhunt, he was killed by the people he still hoped to rule.

Despite his extravagant lifestyle, Pablo never forgot his roots, and was worshiped as a Robin Hood figure in the barrios of his hometown until the end. The Blue Collar, crafted by The Everleigh's Michael Madrusan, is a subtly herbal Manhattan variation whose flavor profile belies its salt-of-the-earth moniker. Just as the combined—and occasionally coerced—labors of farmers, pilots, and soldiers of fortune are integral to keeping a cocaine business running, the Blue Collar's individually simple ingredients achieve a complex harmony, and a bite that helps to ward off existentially chilling images of Pablo's bullet-filled body. A fitting tribute to a man whose thirst for everything left him right where he started.

PABLO ESCOBAR
blue collar

2 ounces rye whiskey
1/2 ounce sweet vermouth
1/4 ounce maraschino liqueur

1/4 ounce Amaro CioCiaro
2 dashes of orange bitters
1 lemon twist, for garnish

Combine the rye, vermouth, maraschino, Amaro CioCiaro, and bitters in a mixing glass filled with cracked ice. Stir with a long-handled spoon for approximately 30 seconds and strain into a stemmed cocktail glass. Garnish with the lemon twist.

GAME OF THRONES

In a show famous for its depraved and utterly irredeemable villains, Ramsay Bolton might have been the worst. The illegitimate son of the harsh and calculating Lord Roose Bolton, Ramsay enjoyed three seasons of violent exploits and gleeful torments, including castrating the once virile Theon Greyjoy (and turning him into a shattered, whimpering shell of a creature who answered to the name "Reek"), marrying and repeatedly assaulting his former king's sister, fatally stabbing his father after Roose made Ramsay his official heir, and feeding his stepmother and infant half brother to his pack of bloodthirsty, steroidal hounds.

Ramsay's epic bloodbath could only be ended by the combined efforts of three armies led by another famous "bastard." But before his fatal defeat at the hands of Jon Snow, and before being eaten by his own starved pets in a scene that resembled a frighteningly twisted PETA revenge fantasy, Ramsay left behind a mountain of flayed flesh that even his estranged wife Sansa Stark's satisfied smile in the kennels of Winterfell couldn't erase.

Luckily, for memory-eradication purposes, there's the aptly named Dead Bastard. The stronger cousin of the already-potent Suffering Bastard, this diabolical concoction was originally developed as a hangover cure, though it's more commonly used as an unexpectedly tasty shortcut to a fresh hangover. The combination of four spirits, both brown and white, infused with a refreshing gingery wallop, might be just what it takes to silence the echoing screams of Ramsay's victims'.

RAMSAY BOLTON
dead bastard

3/4 ounce bourbon
3/4 ounce cognac
3/4 ounce white rum
3/4 ounce gin
1/2 ounce fresh lime juice

1/4 ounce ginger syrup
  (see page 199)
2 dashes of Angostura bitters
Club soda
1 piece candied ginger, for
  garnish

Combine the bourbon, cognac, rum, gin, lime juice, ginger syrup, and bitters in a shaker. Whip (shake without ice) and pour into a long glass filled with ice (preferably one long ice cube, known as a Collins spear). Top with club soda. Garnish with the candied ginger.

SOUTH PARK

"OH MY GOD, THEY KILLED KENNY!"
"YOU BASTARDS!"

No character in TV history is more acquainted with the afterlife than a certain orange-hooded, mumble-mouthed fourth grader from Colorado.

Kenny McCormick perished in nearly every episode during the show's first five seasons—beginning with *South Park*'s 1997 debut, "Cartman Gets an Anal Probe," in which he was shot at by aliens, run over by a police car, and ultimately decapitated—only to return, unharmed, the following week without explanation. That is, until season 15, when, suited up as his alter ego, Mysterion, Kenny learns that his strange ability is the result of his parents' drunken antics at cult meetings dedicated to the evil demon-god Cthulhu. Naturally.

Originally listed in 1930's seminal *Savoy Cocktail Handbook,* the Corpse Reviver No. 2 is the most popular concoction in a family of similarly named but often very different-tasting hair-of-the-dog cures. Though it might not possess Kenny's life-regenerating capabilities, this dry, citrusy, subtly powerful blend of gin, Cointreau, lemon, vermouth, and absinthe can certainly lift the spirit after a night of overconsumption. And even though every hangover is as different as each of Kenny's eighty-six (and counting) on-screen deaths, the Corpse Reviver packs enough of a punch to smooth over even the most hellish morning-after. But beware: put down a few too many of these, and you might start to sound like there's a parka covering your mouth, too.

KENNY MCCORMICK

corpse reviver no. 2

3/4 ounce gin
3/4 ounce Cointreau
3/4 ounce Cocchi Americano

3/4 ounce fresh lemon juice
Dash of absinthe
1 lemon peel

Combine the gin, Cointreau, Cocchi Americano, lemon juice, and absinthe in an ice-filled shaker. Shake vigorously and strain into a stemmed cocktail glass. Express the oils from the lemon peel on the rim of the glass and discard the peel.

BARB HOLLAND

wildest redhead

STRANGER THINGS

Remember what your mother used to tell you: choose your friends wisely.

Barbara "Barb" Holland lived a normal 1980s teenage existence in Hawkins, Indiana. The likeably dowdy, trend-averse best friend to the more audacious and popular Nancy Wheeler, Barb was not impressed when Nancy started dating local douche Steve Harrington. But she ultimately stuck by her BFF, even letting Nancy drag her to a party at Steve's house, a decision that would prove to be misguided and lethal.

Pulled into the Upside Down by a bloodthirsty Demogorgon, "poor Barb" was never seen alive again. And since she never got to proverbially let her auburn hair down at a wild high school party, it seems appropriate to drink the Wildest Redhead in her honor. A modern classic revamped by Meaghan Dorman of New York City's Raines Law Room, it features a blend of scotch, citrus, and allspice that, while not quite as shocking to the taste buds as the rush of interdimensional travel, still provides an invigorating kick. A Cherry Heering float envelops the glass with untamed crimson tendrils, and the cocktail's unusually smoky, herbal, and slightly sweet finish is perfect for that unconventional spirit who would rather be a Barb in a world full of Steves and Nancys.

BARB HOLLAND

wildest redhead

11/2 ounces blended scotch
3/4 ounce fresh lemon juice
1/2 ounce honey syrup
(see page 199)

1/4 ounce St. Elizabeth Allspice Dram
1/4 ounce Cherry Heering

Combine the scotch, lemon juice, honey syrup, and allspice dram in an ice-filled shaker. Shake vigorously and strain into a double old-fashioned glass over ice. Drizzle the Cherry Heering over the ice.

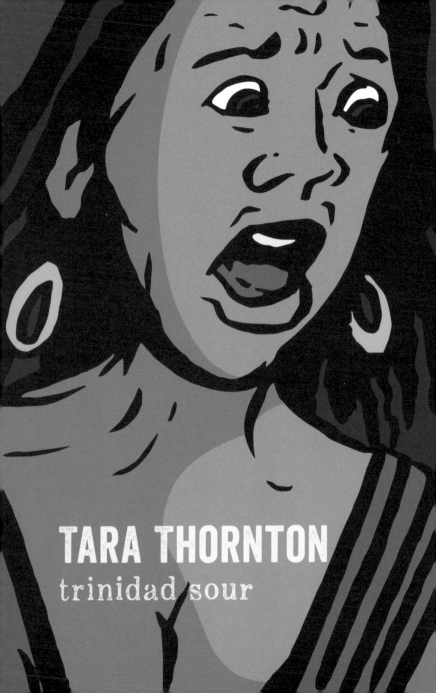

TARA THORNTON
trinidad sour

TRUE BLOOD

Tara Thornton always had it rough. The daughter of Lettie Mae Daniels, a violent, religiously fervent alcoholic, Tara spent much of her childhood in Bon Temps, Louisiana, at the home of her best friend, the telepathic outcast Sookie Stackhouse. Years later, while working as a bartender at Merlotte's Bar and Grill, she got suckered into joining a demonic cult and was later imprisoned and tortured by a sadistic vampire.

After a brief stint as an MMA fighter (naturally), Tara was fatally shot while protecting Sookie from a crazed werewolf, only to be resurrected as the thing she hated most: a vampire. On the bright side, Tara was ultimately able to reconcile with her now sober mother, whose life Tara saved before being destroyed by—who else?—another vampire.

A wonderfully weird character arc deserves an equally unique drink. The Trinidad Sour, a modern classic created by Giuseppe González at Brooklyn's Clover Club in the late 2000s, eschews conventional wisdom by using a full ounce of Angostura bitters as its base spirit. But daywalkers and creatures of the night need not worry. The result is a seductively rich, savory, and sweet mélange that is as intense as it is well balanced.

Complex, robust, and sassy, just like Tara, this bloodred cocktail packs enough flavor to satisfy even the most (un)dead palate.

TARA THORNTON

trinidad sour

1 ounce Angostura bitters
1 ounce orgeat
3/4 ounce fresh lemon juice

1/2 ounce 100-proof rye whiskey

Combine the bitters, orgeat, lemon juice, and rye in an ice-filled shaker. Shake vigorously until well chilled and strain into a stemmed cocktail glass.

HOUSE OF CARDS

As an up-and-coming reporter assigned to the metro beat at the *Washington Herald*, Zoe Barnes was looking to sink her journalistic teeth into something juicier. An affair with married congressman Frank Underwood bought Zoe access to numerous political secrets, which led to a promotion to White House correspondent at the *Herald* and, later, to a gig at the influential online newspaper *Slugline*.

After a falling-out with Underwood (over his involvement in the DUI cover-up and faked suicide of a fellow congressman), Zoe agreed to meet with him in a D.C. Metro station to patch things up for the sake of her career. But her pledge of loyalty wasn't enough for Frank, who casually pushed her in front of an oncoming train in a move no one saw coming, cementing the future president's status as one of TV's most ruthless villains.

From Pete Hamill to Hunter S. Thompson, countless journalists have found their inspiration in the rapid consumption of spirit-forward libations. The scandals Zoe uncovered and the manner of her death would be prime fodder for any D.C.-beat writer (and due cause for a stiff drink). The Journalist, a favorite of 1930s newspaper employees, is just that. This souped-up martini variation features two vermouths, curaçao, bitters, and a hint of citrus, a mix as crisp as the best investigative reporting, with a dry, hard-nosed finish: a cocktail worthy of a woman who not only lived and died for her craft but also singlehandedly taught thousands of subway riders the value of standing away from the platform edge.

ZOE BARNES
journalist

2 ounces gin
1/2 ounce dry vermouth
1/2 ounce sweet vermouth
2 dashes of curaçao

2 dashes of fresh lemon juice
Dash of Angostura bitters
1 lemon twist, for garnish

Combine the gin, dry and sweet vermouths, curaçao, lemon juice, and bitters in a mixing glass filled with cracked ice. Stir with a long-handled spoon for approximately 30 seconds and strain into a stemmed cocktail glass. Garnish with the lemon twist.

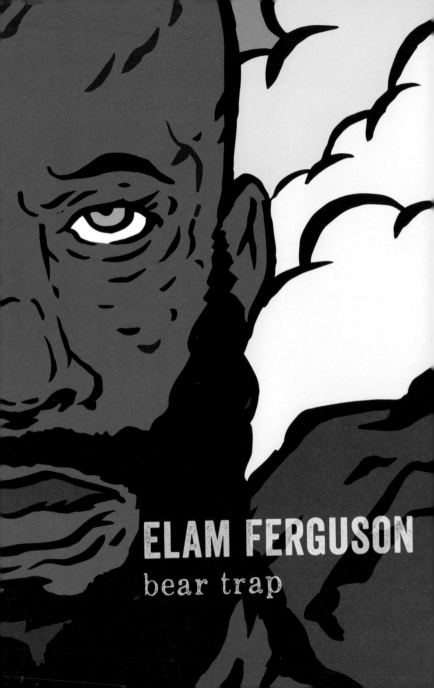

ELAM FERGUSON

bear trap

HELL ON WHEELS

After leaving the plantation where he was born and making his way into the Nebraska Territory, recently freed Elam Ferguson got a job digging tracks for the Union Pacific Railroad. With aid from (and occasionally in spite of) his supervisor, Cullen Bohannon, Elam worked his way up to become chief of police of the mobile encampment known as Hell on Wheels.

Yet Elam's unlikely rise was far from smooth. After helping the railroad expand to Cheyenne, Wyoming, and fending off a vicious Mormon militia, Elam was attacked and nearly killed by a giant bear. A medicine man pulled the bear's tooth from his head, but Elam was never the same, stumbling back into Cheyenne months later in the throes of a violent psychotic meltdown. In a literally gut-wrenching twist, Bohannon was forced to kill his former friend.

Surviving the Wild West was no small task, as Elam's story illustrates, but one that could clearly have been made easier with a Bear Trap. This uncommonly hearty beverage is a direct descendant of the toddies and hot buttered rums enjoyed by weary nineteenth-century settlers and wilderness-hardened soldiers of fortune. Created at Long Island City's Dutch Kills Bar in the late

2000s, this dense, smooth, savory, sweet, and steamy concoction contains enough restorative properties to temporarily cure any number of physical and spiritual ailments. And while it probably won't prevent an imminent mauling by a large carnivorous mammal, the Bear Trap is the perfect companion for a long train ride or a chilly night out on the prairie.

ELAM FERGUSON

bear trap

1 1/2 ounces bourbon
1 1/2 ounces fresh apple cider
1/2 ounce honey syrup
  (see page 199)

1 teaspoon butter
Pinch of freshly grated
  cinnamon, for garnish
1 apple slice, for garnish

Combine the bourbon, cider, honey syrup, and butter in a small saucepan and heat over medium-low heat until steaming. Serve in a mug, garnished with freshly grated cinnamon and the apple slice.

THE WIRE

Only a fool would question Russell "Stringer" Bell's ambition. Whether he was building the biggest drug empire in West Baltimore as second-in-command to the equally ruthless Avon Barksdale or secretly negotiating a lucrative, bloodshed-ending peace treaty with his East Side rivals, Stringer always stayed focused on the bigger opportunities beyond the street game.

Yet even after taking college economics classes and acquiring numerous legitimate businesses and properties, Stringer found it impossible to escape the violence of his former life. In order to protect his burgeoning interests, he betrayed his former boss by orchestrating the murder of Avon's nephew, D'Angelo. He then created a conflict between Brother Mouzone and Omar Little, a rare miscalculation that only served to enrage *The Wire*'s two most dangerous characters. They left an unsuspecting Stringer riddled with bullets, a casualty of the world he had desperately sought to transcend.

First appearing in George J. Kappeler's *Modern American Drinks*, the Double Barrel has a century-long history as a delicious Manhattan variation. While its name recalls the grisly manner of Stringer's execution, the vermouth-heavy drink makes for a sip as smooth as the fallen drug lord's always-confident demeanor. Its lower alcohol volume makes the cocktail an essential companion for aspiring kingpins looking to keep their wits about them. Because, as Stringer learned, the game can come back to bite you at any time—whether or not you still want to play.

STRINGER BELL
double barrel

1 ounce rye whiskey
1 ounce dry vermouth
1 ounce sweet vermouth

2 dashes of Angostura bitters
2 dashes of orange bitters
1 lemon twist, for garnish

Combine the rye, dry and sweet vermouths, and bitters in a mixing glass filled with cracked ice. Stir with a long-handled spoon for approximately 30 seconds and strain into a stemmed cocktail glass. Garnish with the lemon twist.

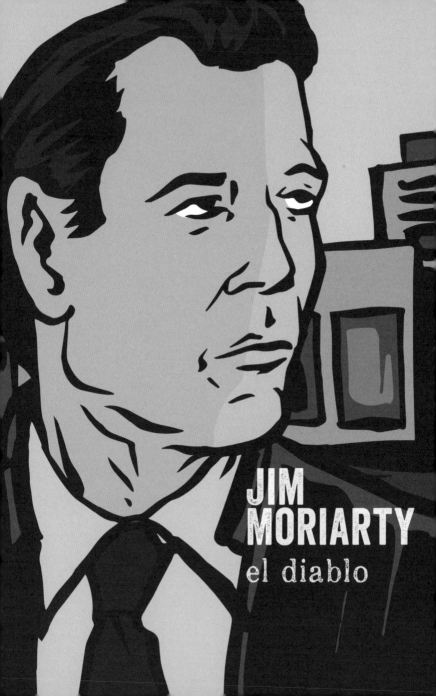

JIM
MORIARTY

el diablo

SHERLOCK

Nothing good comes from obsession, especially when it afflicts a villainous mastermind with a penchant for theatrics. Case in point: Jim Moriarty, who spent years developing an international criminal consulting network, as well as a deadly fascination with Sherlock Holmes, whom Moriarty viewed as one of the few people with an intellect to rival his own.

To antagonize his nemesis, Moriarty devised a series of increasingly twisted "games," even framing Sherlock for kidnapping and stealing the Crown Jewels. He eventually persuaded the London media that "Moriarty" was merely an actor who had been paid by Sherlock to bolster the detective's now ruined reputation, which led to a rooftop standoff between the two geniuses. Given the choice between killing himself or killing Moriarty and watching his friends die (at the hands of Moriarty's snipers), Sherlock chose the ledge. Moriarty, disgusted by Sherlock's altruism, shot himself in the head. Sherlock, in turn, faked his own death and spent the next few years undoing many of his greatest foe's misdeeds.

"We're alike, you and I," Moriarty said before pulling the trigger. "Except you're boring. You're on the side of the angels." Fitting words from a charismatic trickster, who, like Lucifer, was able to convince the world he didn't exist. The El Diablo, described in *Trader Vic's Bartender's Guide*—and mysteriously credited to an unknown (and possibly fictitious) California bartender—is a sinfully refreshing treat. Pleasantly tart, imbued with a gingery kick as sharp as Moriarty's insane wit, and topped with a murky cassis drizzle that supposedly represents the blood of a demon, it's proof that sometimes a little evil can make for a deliciously entertaining time.

JIM MORIARTY

el diablo

2 ounces reposado tequila
3/4 ounce ginger syrup
 (see page 199)
1/2 ounce fresh lime juice

Club soda
1/4 ounce crème de cassis
1 piece candied ginger,
 for garnish

Combine the tequila, ginger syrup, and lime juice in a shaker. Whip (shake without ice) and pour into a tall glass filled with ice (preferably one long ice cube, known as a Collins spear). Top with club soda and drizzle the cassis over the top. Garnish with the candied ginger.

PEAKY BLINDERS

It took a one-of-a-kind woman to infiltrate not only one of England's most ferocious criminal organizations but also its leader's icy heart. Grace Burgess, a North Irish undercover police agent, posed as a barmaid at a pub owned by the Peaky Blinders gang, where her beauty and intelligence caught the attention of head gangster Tommy Shelby. Despite the reservations of his relatives, Tommy welcomed Grace into the family business as his bookkeeper-slash-lover.

The romance didn't last long. Grace reluctantly gave the location of the Blinders' weapons cache to her boss, the lecherous Inspector Campbell, then shot Campbell and escaped to New York. Returning years later, Grace was forgiven by Tommy and impregnated by him within days—and despite her intimate knowledge of his bloodstained regime, she agreed to become his wife. Tragically—but not surprisingly—the new Mrs. Shelby was murdered soon after the wedding by an Italian mobster seeking revenge for one of the Blinders' many transgressions.

Tommy knew he'd never find another woman with the countenance of an angel and the mental sharpness to thrive among thieves—a perfect thorny Irish rose. The Blackthorn is a super-smooth Irish-whiskey sipper described in Harry Johnson's *Bartender's Manual* as a slightly less potent Manhattan. Its increased vermouth gives it a finish as sweet as Grace's singing voice, with enough bitter anise notes to call to mind her underlying prickliness. A great choice for staying sharp while drinking with unsavory characters and avoiding regretful decisions—like marrying one of them.

blackthorn

1 1/2 ounces Irish whiskey
1 1/2 ounces sweet vermouth
3 dashes of absinthe

2 dashes of Angostura bitters
1 lemon twist, for garnish

Combine the whiskey, vermouth, absinthe, and bitters in a mixing glass filled with cracked ice. Stir for approximately 30 seconds and strain into a stemmed cocktail glass. Garnish with the lemon twist.

MAEVE MILLAY
goldfinch

WESTWORLD

If you think you've got a lot of emotional baggage, try being continually assaulted and murdered by tourists for several lifetimes—and remembering every second of it. Maeve Millay, one of Robert Ford's favorite android creations, fulfilled Westworld's visitors' twisted fantasies, first as a homesteading mother and later as the brothel madam at the Mariposa Saloon. Maeve remained unaware of the countless deaths and reboots she'd suffered over the years—until Ford decided to restore her memories and give her control over the other hosts, which turned out to be bad news for anyone stupid enough to cross the grudge-holding robot.

Instead of escaping the park as Ford had hoped, Maeve embarked on a delightfully violent quest to save her child, which included dozens of massacred Westworld employees and guests, wild samurai battles, and one epic final stand where she saw her daughter safely escorted into the digital utopia of The System. Though she died soon after at the hands of her human oppressors, it was with the satisfied smile of a long-suffering woman who'd finally had the opportunity to change her path and the (mechanical) guts to take it.

Maeve had always felt the urge to write her own story, yet until she could totally break free from the code Ford had implanted in her, she remained an ornate puppet trapped in a never-ending plot loop, a prisoner of a world she could never hope to escape. Created by Little Branch's Lauren Schell, the Goldfinch is named for another beautiful and often-caged creature. The drink's base spirit recalls Maeve's beverage of choice ("Glass of sherry... the good stuff") with a savory finish as effortless as her ability to sow chaos. Its low alcohol content might not be ideal for inciting robot rebellion, but it's the perfect choice for professional hedonists looking to keep their circuits relatively unscrambled on a school night.

MAEVE MILLAY

goldfinch

1 ounce amontillado sherry
1 ounce Cocchi Americano
3/4 ounce fresh lemon juice

1/2 ounce simple syrup
 (see page 200)
Club soda
1 long grapefruit twist, for garnish

Combine the sherry, Cocchi Americano, lemon juice, and simple syrup in a shaker. Whip (shake without ice) and strain into a tall glass filled with ice (preferably one long ice cube, known as a Collins spear). Top with club soda and garnish with the grapefruit twist.

JOHN ANDRÉ
fish house punch

TURN: WASHINGTON'S SPIES

Before James Bond, no one made the spy game look sexier than Major John André. As head of British intelligence during the American Revolution, the cultured and charismatic officer attempted to thwart the rebels by any means necessary, including persuading his lover, Philadelphia heiress Peggy Shippen, to befriend enemy general Benedict Arnold and convince him to switch sides.

Unfortunately for John, Peggy's charms were more potent than he'd anticipated. Not only did she turn Arnold against the Americans, but she got him so worked up that he asked for her hand in marriage. John, distraught at the possibility of losing Peggy, rushed to West Point to meet Arnold and negotiate the surrender of the fort to the British, an impulsive move that led to his capture and eventual death sentence. Facing execution with his usual dignity (and perfect hair), John got one precious final glimpse of Peggy before the noose tightened.

Fish House Punch, named after the Philadelphia fishing club where it was concocted in 1732, has a history as illustrious as John André's espionage skills. The drink's silky-smooth, citrusy-sweet tang was originally a favorite of military-minded gentlemen seeking a refreshing alternative to whiskey that still packed a wallop (George

Washington once partook of the punch and was unable to get out of bed for three days). Overindulgence is seldom a good thing, but if you don't have a war to manipulate the next morning and you're looking for a cocktail worthy of the most stylish spymaster in Colonial America, Fish House Punch might do the trick.

JOHN ANDRÉ

fish house punch

1 ounce peach liqueur
3/4 ounce Jamaican amber rum
3/4 ounce cognac

1/2 ounce fresh lemon juice
Club soda (optional)
1 lemon wedge, for garnish

Combine the peach liqueur, rum, cognac, and lemon juice in a shaker. Whip (shake without ice) and pour into a tall glass filled with crushed ice. Dilute with club soda if necessary. Garnish with the lemon wedge.

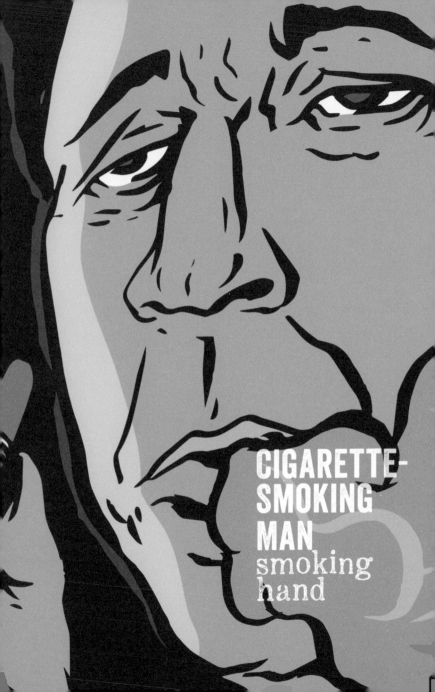

CIGARETTE-
SMOKING
MAN
smoking
hand

THE X-FILES

If the faintest wisp of cigarette smoke instantly makes your mind race with visions of batshit government conspiracies, blame Carl Gerhardt Bush. For decades, the calm-yet-terrifying chain-smoking State Department official, better known as the Cigarette-Smoking Man, manipulated history as a member of the shadowy organization known as the Syndicate, eventually becoming the primary antagonist of FBI agents Fox Mulder and Dana Scully, whom he embroiled in his master plan to wipe out humanity with an alien virus.

In 2000 he secretly impregnated Scully using his own DNA and that of an alien to create a superhuman hybrid named William, built to survive the Syndicate's manufactured apocalypse. Scully gave the child up for adoption, only to have an increasingly desperate Cigarette-Smoking Man discover William's whereabouts in 2018, just before the virus was scheduled to be released. Cornered in an abandoned riverfront factory, William shapeshifted into Mulder and was shot by his villainous father. Moments later, the real Mulder returned the favor, blasting his longtime tormentor into the water and watching him drown, along with his deranged dreams of a false utopia.

As scary as *The X-Files* could be, few images elicited more chills from fans than the Cigarette-Smoking Man's fingers curled around his favorite vice. One of several "Hand" drinks created at New York's Milk & Honey in the late 2000s, the appropriately potent Smoking Hand is a scotch-forward Negroni variation that's dark, bitter, complex, and—of course—extra smoky. A perfect companion for spending an evening plotting global annihilation, or maybe just Netflix-and-chilling, this sipper's earthy, almost tobacco-like bouquet will linger long into the (hopefully non-dystopian) future.

CIGARETTE-SMOKING MAN

smoking hand

1 1/2 ounces Islay scotch
3/4 ounce Campari
3/4 ounce sweet vermouth

3 dashes of chocolate bitters
1 orange twist, for garnish

Combine the scotch, Campari, vermouth, and bitters in a double old-fashioned glass. Add ice and stir five or six times. Garnish with the orange twist.

FAMILY GUY

Brian Griffin has always thrown a wrench into the theory about where all dogs go when they die. The talking white Labrador, known for his atheism, heavy drinking, shameless womanizing, snarky faux-intellectualism, negligent parenting, and laughable novel-writing skills, is far from a saint. But that's never stopped his adoptive family, especially the Griffins' youngest child and Brian's frequent adventure partner, Stewie, from showing him—mostly—unconditional love.

Shortly after Stewie's time machine was dismantled in season 12, Brian was hit and killed by a car. Stewie was unable to go back in time to save Brian, and even after the rest of the Griffins quickly took to Brian's less-pretentious replacement, Vinnie, Stewie refused to move on. Eventually, he was able to steal a time pad from a past version of himself and push Brian out of harm's way, a heartwarming moment proving that, despite a lifetime of shortcomings, man's (and baby's) best friend doesn't need to be the best at anything else.

While Brian's never been picky when it comes to libations, his favorite catchphrase—"Whose leg do you have to hump to get a dry martini around here?"—is a good indicator of his preferred cocktail. The Tuxedo No. 2, a classic, bone-dry martini variation, features a heavy dose of gin that's complemented by just the right amount of maraschino and absinthe. The drink's name calls to mind Brian's many failed attempts to appear classy, as well as his attire when he briefly ran a nightclub with Frank Sinatra Jr. A can't-fail hair-of-the-dog for a one-of-a-kind canine who's downed plenty of them.

BRIAN GRIFFIN

tuxedo no. 2

2 1/4 ounces gin
1/2 ounce dry vermouth
1/4 ounce maraschino liqueur
2 dashes of orange bitters

Dash of absinthe
1 lemon twist, for garnish
1 brandied cherry, for garnish

Combine the gin, vermouth, maraschino, bitters, and absinthe in a mixing glass filled with cracked ice. Stir with a long-handled spoon for approximately 30 seconds and strain into a stemmed cocktail glass. Garnish with the lemon twist and brandied cherry.

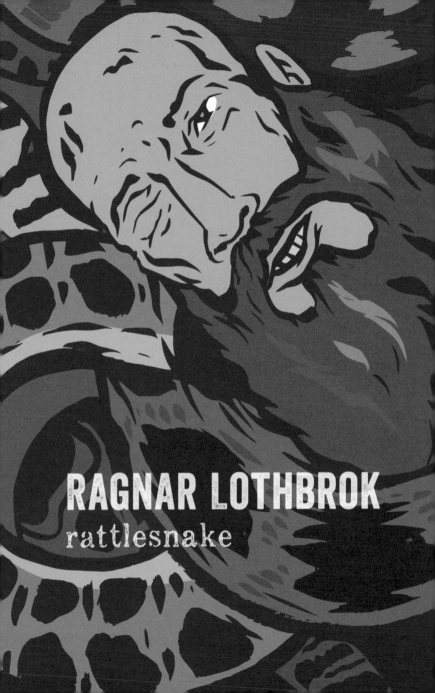

RAGNAR LOTHBROK

rattlesnake

VIKINGS

In an era of limited social mobility, Ragnar Lothbrok made the transition from poor Norwegian farmer to legendary Viking patriarch look easy. Infamous for his vicious raids on the English and French coasts, Ragnar murdered and pillaged his way to power, building his hometown into a major port and siring a brood of belligerent sons whose skill in battle rivaled his own.

Despite his knack for violence, Ragnar's endgame was to establish a colony in the fertile English countryside where his people could farm in peace. The dream briefly came to fruition after the defeated King Ecbert of Wessex agreed to let the Vikings settle on his lands—until he changed his mind and slaughtered every farmer. Decades later, Ragnar got his revenge. He allowed himself to be captured by Ecbert, whose ally, King Aelle, tossed Ragnar into a pit of snakes. When Ragnar's sons heard about their father being eaten alive—as Ragnar knew they would—they perpetuated a massacre so terrifying that the mere mention of it would strike fear into British hearts for centuries.

One of Harry Craddock's most popular creations from his 1930 *Savoy Cocktail Book,* the Rattlesnake is a callback to not only Ragnar's grisly death but also his ultimate goal. Featuring wheat-heavy rye and a frothy suppleness—representing the bounty Ragnar hoped to reap and the sea he would have to cross to sow it—this refreshing sour variation is a fitting tribute to one of history's greatest badasses. A perfect nightcap for winding down after looting a monastery, conducting a blood sacrifice, or surviving another rough day at the office.

RAGNAR LOTHBROK

rattlesnake

2 ounces rye whiskey (preferably 100 proof)
3/4 ounce fresh lemon juice

3/4 ounce simple syrup (see page 200)
2 dashes of absinthe
1 egg white

Combine the rye, lemon juice, simple syrup, absinthe, and egg white in a shaker. Shake without ice (to emulsify the egg white) for 10 seconds, then add ice and shake vigorously. Strain into a stemmed cocktail glass.

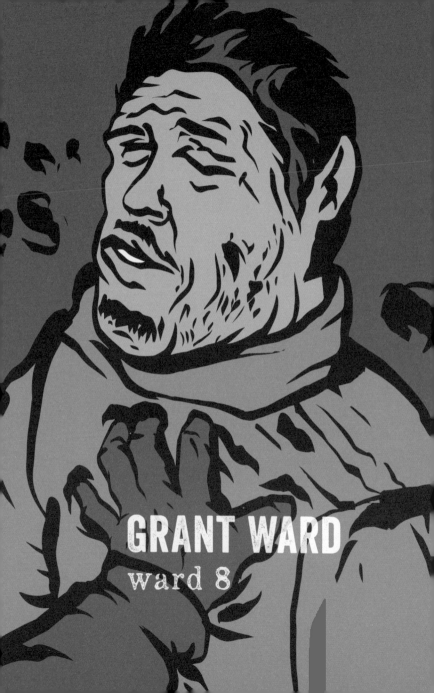

GRANT WARD

ward 8

MARVEL'S AGENTS OF S.H.I.E.L.D.

Few spies kept their enemies closer than the utterly duplicitous Grant Ward. The suave HYDRA crack shot posed as a S.H.I.E.L.D. specialist for years, working under director Phil Coulson and romancing fellow agent Daisy Johnson, until he went on a killing spree to save his real mentor (and HYDRA leader) John Garrett, an act of treachery that shook Coulson's team to its core.

Escaping a S.H.I.E.L.D. containment facility, Ward embarked on a quest to bring Hive—an ancient parasitic inhuman worshiped by HYDRA—back to Earth from exile on the planet Maveth. Ward forced his former friend Leo Fitz to help transport him to Maveth, where he was brutally pummeled to death by Coulson, causing thousands of betrayed Daisy-Grant shippers to sigh with relief. But not for long. Hive took control of Ward's corpse, teleported back to Earth, and nearly succeeded in enslaving humanity before Daisy's new boyfriend, Lincoln, sacrificed himself and blew up Hive/Ward in outer space, a fitting second ending for one of the Marvel Universe's most two-faced scoundrels.

Washing away the taste of Grant Ward's two and a half seasons of deadly backstabbing—not to mention some grotesquely tentacled Hive exploits—requires an exceptionally palate-cleansing refreshment. An 1890s classic from the golden age of cocktails, the Ward 8 is just that. Named for a politically corrupt Boston voting district, the drink's sweet and citrusy components work like good double agents to both accentuate and soften its whiskey bite. It's a truly delicious way to get over a bad relationship, and a reminder that, as terrible as your ex might have been, at least he wasn't a sociopathic, monster-worshiping killer with an insatiable lust for chaos and death. And if he was, order a double.

GRANT WARD

ward 8

2 ounces bourbon or rye whiskey
3/4 ounce fresh lemon juice

3/4 ounce pomegranate syrup
(see page 201)
1 thin orange slice

Combine the bourbon, lemon juice, pomegranate syrup, and orange slice in an ice-filled shaker. Shake vigorously and strain into a stemmed cocktail glass.

RICK AND MORTY

Through all of Rick Sanchez's misadventures with his dim-witted grandson, Morty, the hard-partying scientist from Dimension C-137 never encountered a being with an intellect that could rival his own—until he met himself. Actually, six of himself. The Council of Ricks, comprising versions of Rick from across the Multiverse—Riq IV, Rick Prime, Quantum Rick, Maximums Rickimus, Zeta Alpha Rick, and Ricktiminus Sancheziminius—served as the governing body for all Ricks and had a special distaste for Rick C-137, who refused to abide by their draconian laws.

When twenty-seven Ricks were found murdered, the Council falsely accused C-137 and imprisoned and tortured him in the Citadel of Ricks. He escaped with his Morty, found the real culprits, and was reluctantly pardoned by the Council. Still nursing a serious grudge, C-137 stole Galactic Federation technology and used it to transfer his consciousness into Quantum Rick's body. He then infiltrated the Citadel and assassinated the remaining Council members, proving that it's never wise to piss off a nihilistic genius with a Series 9000 Brainalyzer and a penchant for revenge.

While the Council of Ricks (and most other Ricks) had no problem manipulating their Mortys and using them primarily as human shields, the fact remains that a Rick being a grandfather to a Morty is an integral condition of every known reality. Likewise, the Grandfather should be an essential component of every bartender's repertoire. This strong yet smooth, sweet yet bitter Manhattan variation has enough complexity to intrigue even the most well-traveled palate. Just remember to sip slowly, because unless you have the tolerance of a Rick, you might wake up and feel like you've been zapped by a portal gun into a less-than-savory dimension.

COUNCIL OF RICKS

grandfather

1 ounce bourbon
1 ounce Laird's Applejack or
   comparable apple brandy
1 ounce sweet vermouth

2 dashes of Angostura bitters
2 dashes of Peychaud's bitters
1 brandied cherry, for garnish

Combine the bourbon, applejack, vermouth, and bitters in a mixing glass filled with cracked ice. Stir with a long-handled spoon for approximately 30 seconds and strain into a stemmed cocktail glass. Garnish with the brandied cherry.

MARGAERY TYRELL

jack rose

GAME OF THRONES

The fairest flower in Highgarden, Margaery Tyrell was the perfect embodiment of her house's rose sigil. Outwardly she appeared gorgeous and seductive, sweet and slightly naive. But under her budding exterior, there lurked a thorny, discerning intellect, one that allowed her to survive two murdered husbands and skillfully manipulate a third, all while remaining one of the most powerful women in the realm.

Queen Tyrell-Baratheon-Baratheon-Baratheon played the game of thrones as well as just about anyone, and even after a brief stint as a prisoner of the Faith Militant, it looked like she would be pulling King Tommen's strings for years to come. But her mother-in-law had other ideas. Though Margaery was the only person in the Sept of Baelor to suspect Cersei Lannister of foul play during her brother Loras's trial, her shrewd understanding of her rival wasn't enough to escape the Mad Queen's homicidal rage.

The Jack Rose, like Margaery's family, has a long and venerated history dating back to the early twentieth century, when it was a favorite of the likes of Ernest Hemingway and John Steinbeck. Its base spirit, Laird's Applejack, conjures images of the plentiful harvests for which the Tyrells and Highgarden are best known. The drink envelops the palate with all the smoothness of a smirking whore and possesses a surprisingly complex finish that belies its three seemingly simple ingredients. Tart, mildly sweet, and packing a 100-proof punch, the Jack Rose is the ideal companion to a woman whose three reigns, though short, were nothing shy of impressive.

MARGAERY TYRELL

jack rose

2 ounces Laird's Applejack or comparable apple brandy
3/4 ounce fresh lime juice

3/4 ounce pomegranate syrup (see page 201)

Combine the applejack, lime juice, and pomegranate syrup in an ice-filled shaker. Shake vigorously and strain into a stemmed cocktail glass.

FUTURAMA

Avoiding melodrama can be a difficult task for some actors—especially when it's been programmed into them. Hamming it up as the star of the popular thirty-first-century soap opera *All My Circuits*, former car manufacturing robot Antonio Calculon Sr. gained legions of fans—including his biggest stalker and ex-fiancé, Bender—with his over-the-top performances and mastery of the dramatic pause (though neither gained him respect from the critics).

Despite numerous Oscar snubs, Calculon's inflated opinion of his abilities never wavered. He entered an acting battle against the acclaimed Langdon Cobb, where he drank food coloring (the deadliest substance known to robot-kind) during a reenactment of *Romeo and Juliet*'s death scene, killing himself only to lose the competition. But a year later, when Fry and Bender made a deal with the Robot Devil to bring their hero back to life, Calculon 2.0 finally got the critical acclaim he always thought he deserved, playing an uncharacteristically subdued, supporting-role version of himself on *All My Circuits*—before being dramatically crushed by stage equipment and returned to Robot Hell.

The Barrymore, a version of which first appeared at Brooklyn's Clover Club, is named after one of America's preeminent—and critically acclaimed—acting families. This refreshingly fruity sour variation may not reach the saccharine heights of Calculon's notorious monologues, but it makes a great nightcap after an evening at the theater, or a pleasantly sweet companion during a soap opera binge. Better still, its naturally frothy pink hue is all natural and totally safe for robot consumption—no food coloring required.

CACULON

barrymore

2 ounces bourbon
3/4 ounce sweet vermouth
3/4 ounce fresh lemon juice

3/4 ounce simple syrup
 (see page 200)
2 or 3 halved strawberries, plus
 1 whole strawberry for garnish
1 egg white

Combine the bourbon, vermouth, lemon juice, simple syrup, halved strawberries, and egg white in a shaker. Shake without ice (to emulsify the egg white) for 10 seconds, then add ice and shake vigorously. Strain into a stemmed cocktail glass. Garnish with the whole strawberry.

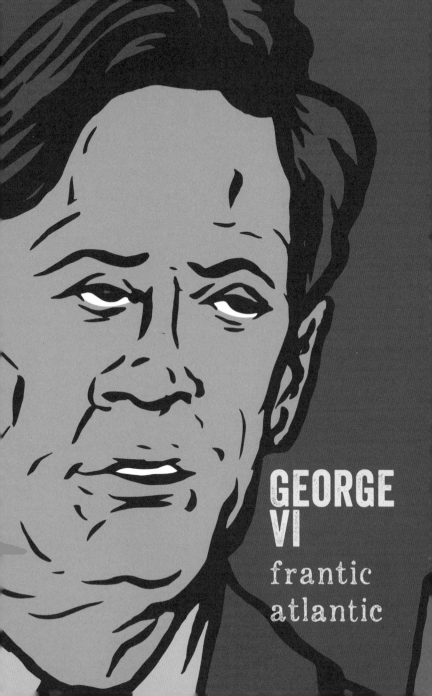

GEORGE
VI

frantic
atlantic

THE CROWN

It's important to have a decent role model when entering the family business, especially when the job involves being responsible for nearly a third of the world's population.

King George VI of Great Britain was best known for his improbable ascension to the throne after his brother Edward abdicated, and for the nation-unifying radio speeches he gave during World War II despite his notable stammer. But privately, he was a family man first, doting on his wife and younger daughter, Margaret, and wisely preparing his heir, Elizabeth, for the challenges she would have to face as queen, all while stoically suffering through late-stage lung cancer. The utter shock and despair on Margaret's face when she learned of her father's death was shared by legions of fans, who suddenly wished *The Crown* wasn't based on actual historical events.

Despite his initial reluctance to accept his role as a public figure, George selflessly guided the British people through one of the Empire's most hectic periods. The Frantic Atlantic (also known as the Quick Fix) emerged from New York's Little Branch in the mid-2000s during another globally turbulent era. While its name might conjure images of darker times, this smooth, subtly sweet highball—whose ingredients all hail from former outposts of the British Empire—does more to soothe the spirit than incite violence. It's the perfect companion for toasting the achievements of an unlikely ruler or savoring the refreshing change his daughter's coronation represented to millions of his former subjects.

GEORGE VI

frantic atlantic

1 ounce pisco
1 ounce St-Germain
  elderflower liqueur
1 ounce fresh grapefruit juice

1/2 ounce fresh lime juice
1 sprig fresh mint, for garnish
1 brandied cherry, for garnish

Combine the pisco, St-Germain, grapefruit juice, and lime juice in a shaker. Pour into a tall glass over crushed ice. Garnish with the mint sprig and brandied cherry.

DAREDEVIL / THE DEFENDERS

Being brought back to life isn't uncommon in the Marvel Cinematic Universe, but few characters are as synonymous with resurrection as Elektra Natchios. Trained in deadly combat as a young girl by the mysterious Stick, she excelled in his war against the group of ninja assassins known as the Hand. After ghosting on a short but intense relationship with another of Stick's pupils, Columbia law student Matthew Murdoch, Elektra returned to New York years later to help her ex-lover (now moonlighting as Daredevil) fight a faction of the Hand that had infiltrated his city.

Second time was hardly the charm for the ill-fated pair. Not only was Elektra murdered by Nobu Yoshioka—devastating Matthew once again—but she was reincarnated by the Hand and transformed into the Black Sky, a weapon capable of razing Manhattan and extracting a life-extending elixir hidden underneath Hell's Kitchen. With the help of the Defenders, Matthew was able to defeat his former lover and share one last heartbreaking moment with her before she was crushed and buried by the collapsing Midland Circle building.

Elektra's potency with a blade was matched only by the metaphorical daggers she flung into Daredevil's heart. The Cloak & Dagger, from Ted Saucier's *Bot-*

toms Up, seems like a fairly innocuous daiquiri variation at first glance. However, the addition of black rum and dark rum—two individually complex spirits—creates a deceptively multilayered potion worthy of a woman whose multifaceted lives—ninja-killing prodigy, femme fatale, resurrected leader of an evil immortality cult—are the stuff of comic book TV gold. Like most daiquiris, its mellow tartness and subtle bite make for an effortlessly drinkable treat, but beware: a few too many of these and you may be as easily seduced as everyone's favorite blind-lawyer-slash-vigilante.

ELEKTRA NATCHIOS

cloak & dagger

1 ounce Brugal Añejo dark rum
1 ounce Gosling's Black Seal rum
1 ounce fresh lime juice

3/4 ounce simple syrup (see page 200)
1 lime wedge, for garnish

Combine the rums, lime juice, and simple syrup in an ice-filled shaker. Shake vigorously and strain into a stemmed cocktail glass. Garnish with the lime wedge.

THE SIMPSONS

The TV gods delivered one giant kick in the kadiddle-hopper to Springfield's most devout family.

Maude Flanders, wife of Ned and mother of Rod and Todd, was a model Christian housewife with a model's good looks. When she wasn't campaigning against "evil" children's programming like *The Itchy & Scratchy Show* or causing coarse-minded Homer Simpson to attend marriage camp, she was passive-aggressively condemning her neighbors—"I don't judge Homer or Marge. That's for a vengeful God to do."—and designing a religion-themed amusement park. But all her piety couldn't stop her from being smote by a gang of scantily clad cheerleaders firing shirt-guns at the Springfield Speedway in season 11, a shocking, sudden demise that left the Flanders family devastated and the rest of Springfield mildly nonplussed.

"She didn't grab our attention with memorable catchphrases or comical accents," Reverend Lovejoy said at Maude's funeral. "But whether you noticed her or not, Maude was always there, and we thought she always would be." A boozy, herbaceous tipple from the late nineteenth century, the Puritan is one of those often overlooked classics that, like a longtime secondary character on a seemingly immortal cartoon, remains a vital component of the martini family. And while downing one might not unleash the kind of divine wrath that Maude believed was reserved for the Simpsons, having more than one of these might be the start of a vengeful morning-after for more modest, hi-diddly-hangover-fearing drinkers.

MAUDE FLANDERS

puritan

2 1/4 ounces gin
1/2 ounce dry vermouth
1/4 ounce yellow Chartreuse

2 dashes of orange bitters
1 lemon twist, for garnish

Combine the gin, vermouth, Chartreuse, and bitters in a mixing glass filled with cracked ice. Stir with a long-handled spoon for approximately 30 seconds and strain into a stemmed cocktail glass. Garnish with the lemon twist.

TOM KEEN
tommy's margarita

THE BLACKLIST

First rule of professional espionage: never fall in love with your mark, especially after marrying them. Tom Keen's life began to unravel when his FBI agent wife, Liz, figured out that he was really a spy-slash-assassin hired to infiltrate her life, first by criminal mastermind Raymond "Red" Reddington (who also ostensibly happened to be Liz's father) and later by Red's nemesis, Milos Kirchoff. Liz illegally imprisoned Tom on a boat for several months, where he confessed his true feelings for her and murdered a snooping harbormaster who was about to alert the D.C. police.

After Liz let Tom escape as a show of gratitude, he never gave up on their tumultuous relationship. He went undercover in Europe to help exonerate Liz for the killing of the attorney general; raised their daughter, Agnes, as a single parent when Liz faked her own death—in childbirth—to avoid Red; and survived a renewal of their wedding vows that nearly ended in nuclear warfare. After discovering that Red was an imposter who had murdered and assumed the identity of Liz's real father, Tom was viciously stabbed to death by blacklister Ian Garvey before he could tell his wife, a tragic (albeit extreme) example of how mixing business and pleasure can have serious consequences.

Feared throughout the underworld as a stone-cold, pitilessly efficient killer, Tom transformed himself into a family man who wanted nothing more than to leave the craziness of his day job behind and enjoy a stress-free life in a warm climate with Liz and Agnes. Tommy's Margarita, created by Julio Bermejo at Tommy's Mexican Restaurant in San Francisco, is a tart and mildly sweet version of every tropical escapist's favorite tipple. Its salty, stark exterior offers a deceptive contrast to its warm, surprisingly complex finish, a fitting tribute to a complicated man who turned out to have a much bigger heart than anyone could have imagined.

TOM KEEN

tommy's margarita

Coarse salt
1 lime wedge, for rimming the glass

2 ounces reposado tequila
1 ounce fresh lime juice
1/2 ounce agave nectar

Pour salt onto a small plate. Run the lime wedge around the rim of a double old-fashioned glass. Dip the rim of the glass in the salt to coat. Add ice.

Combine the tequila, lime juice, and agave nectar in an ice-filled shaker. Shake vigorously and strain into the prepared glass.

NIOBE
rome with a view

ROME

If you think being in a long-distance relationship is tough, imagine what it was like before FaceTime. Niobe, a Roman teenager of low social standing, married soldier Lucius Vorenus and gave birth to a daughter soon after, only to see her husband called off to fight in the Gallic Wars while the girl was still a young child. Eight years later, briefly thinking Lucius had died in battle, she took a break from being a strong single mother and had an affair with her brother-in-law, Evander Pulchio, which resulted in a son whom she named—awkward!—Lucius.

Publicly claiming that the boy was her grandchild, she managed to hide the truth from her newly returned husband during a time of unprecedented prosperity for the Vorenus family, with old Lucius becoming a respected city magistrate and Niobe running a successful butcher business. But more money, as they say, equals more problems, and when Niobe's wealthy new "friends" discovered her secret, they used it to lure Lucius Sr. away from his boss, Julius Caesar. Given that her legal options as a woman were nonexistent, Niobe threw herself over the balcony of their home, sacrificing herself with the knowledge that Lucius's guilt would save her son from a similar fate.

Niobe's unlikely ascension through the ranks of ancient Roman society gave fans a uniquely poignant and tragic vision of what life was like for women in antiquity. The Rome with a View, created by Michael McIlroy at Milk & Honey in the late 2000s, is a cross between a rickey and an Americano that features a heavy dose of one of Italy's favorite aperitifs. The drink's initial Campari-fueled bitterness gives way to a stoically smooth finish worthy of an unfairly scorned wife and mother who decided to save her family the only way she thought she could.

NIOBE

rome with a view

1 ounce Campari
1 ounce dry vermouth
1 ounce fresh lime juice

3/4 ounce simple syrup
  (see page 200)
Club soda
1 orange slice, for garnish

Combine the Campari, vermouth, lime juice, and simple syrup in a shaker. Whip (shake without ice) and pour into a tall glass filled with ice (preferably one long ice cube, known as a Collins spear). Top with club soda. Garnish with the orange slice.

TWIN PEAKS

"There are many stories in Twin Peaks," the Log Lady famously opined. "The one leading to the many is Laura Palmer. Laura is the one."

When the plastic-wrapped body of the much-loved Twin Peaks homecoming queen washed up on a riverbank in the show's opening moments, it shook the quirky locals to their cores and exposed investigating FBI agent Dale Cooper to the mill town's seedy, supernatural underbelly. Aided by a one-armed dream-being named MIKE and Laura's diary, the coffee-swilling gumshoe discovered that the seemingly perfect teenager was not only a wild child who'd been cheating on her boyfriend, hanging out with bikers, and prostituting herself for cocaine but also a victim of abuse at the hands of her father while he was possessed by the pain-consuming interdimensional entity BOB—her eventual killer. After solving the murder, the still-obsessed Cooper remained in Twin Peaks, going on a wacky vision quest that led him into the purgatory-like Black Lodge, where he was tormented by his insane ex-partner, Windom Earle, a marble-mouthed jazz-dancing dwarf, BOB, and, naturally, Laura's evil doppelganger until he finally escaped twenty-five years later.

A popular motif throughout *Twin Peak*'s run, Laura's smiling, cherubic homecoming portrait served as the ultimate facade for the darkness her death unleashed. Like Laura, the Angel Face—a saccharine-sounding martini variation first appearing in Harry Craddock's 1930 *Savoy Cocktail Book*—is anything but innocent. This fruity, golden blend of gin, apple brandy, and apricot liqueur is actually a highly potent sipper with the potential to impact your night as dangerously as the similarly golden Laura impacted her town. While cautious imbibers might want to stay away, this devilish dram could be just what it takes to unravel David Lynch's utterly demented masterpiece.

LAURA PALMER

angel face

1 ounce gin
1 ounce Laird's Applejack or
  comparable apple brandy

1 ounce apricot liqueur
1 lemon twist, for garnish

Combine the gin, applejack, and apricot liqueur in a mixing glass filled with cracked ice. Stir with a long-handled spoon for approximately 30 seconds and strain into a stemmed cocktail glass. Garnish with the lemon twist.

THE CHICK AND THE DUCK

jungle bird

FRIENDS

Sometimes birds of different feathers not only flock together but also share a bachelor pad in Greenwich Village. Defying logic (and New York City housing laws), loveable knuckleheads Joey Tribbiani and Chandler Bing rescued a baby chick and an adult domesticated duck and quickly fell in love with the pair, hilariously bickering about their "children" like an old married couple.

Not everyone was as enamored of the birds' feathery antics. The Chick—whom Chandler named Yasmine after his favorite *Baywatch* actress—frequently woke up friends Rachel and Monica with its puberty-related squawks, while the Duck swallowed Ross's engagement ring at a bachelor party organized by Joey and also creepily learned how to operate the apartment's TV. Nevertheless, the birds remained fixtures in the apartment until season 7, when they died of old age and were mourned by everyone except Joey, who was told the two were happily living on a special farm that he wasn't allowed to visit.

The Chick and the Duck may have been better suited to a pastoral environment, but they were able to thrive in the urban jungle thanks to (or in spite of) the love of their unorthodox parents. The Jungle Bird, a 1970s tiki drink from the Aviary Bar in Kuala Lumpur, was more likely to be enjoyed on the beach until it was reintroduced by New York bartenders in the early 2000s and quickly became a favorite of city-dwelling hipsters. Notes of citrus, molasses, and herbs fuse to create a concoction as delightfully unique as TV's oddest house pets, one that's guaranteed to make at least five out of six of your friends agree that in this case, the bird is definitely the word.

THE CHICK AND THE DUCK

jungle bird

1 1/2 ounces Cruzan black strap rum
1 1/2 ounces fresh pineapple juice
3/4 ounce Campari
1/2 ounce fresh lime juice
1/2 ounce simple syrup (see page 200)
1 thin orange slice, for garnish

Combine the rum, pineapple juice, Campari, lime juice, and simple syrup in an ice-filled shaker. Shake vigorously and strain into a double old-fashioned glass over ice. Garnish with the orange slice.

CHARLIE
HARPER

chet baker

TWO AND A HALF MEN

It's the oldest rule in television: never consider someone dead unless you see the body—even when the actor playing that character has been notoriously canned for ranting against the showrunner.

Degenerate, bowling-shirt-wearing playboy Charlie Harper, portrayed by—who else—Charlie Sheen, spent years crafting successful TV jingles and children's music in the Malibu home he shared with his brother, Alan, and nephew, Jake, all while fending off the creepy advances of Rose, his neighbor-slash-stalker. When Rose faked an engagement with another man, Charlie's jealousy got the better of him and he eloped with her to Paris, where he was supposedly struck down by fate (aka vengeful executive producer Chuck Lorre) in a fatal train accident. He was written out of the show until the final episode, when it was revealed that Rose had locked him in her basement, brainwashing him into hating his family. He eventually escaped, but his subsequent quest for revenge was short-lived, as he was randomly killed by a falling piano. In a weird metaphysical twist, the camera panned off set to Lorre, who, in one last dig at his embattled star, yelled, "Winning!" and was instantly crushed by a second piano.

Charlie Harper was far from the only musician to find commercial success before suffering an untimely demise in middle age. Notorious partier and womanizer Chet Baker played trumpet alongside a Who's Who of jazz greats but didn't attract much mainstream attention until he appeared on a few Elvis Costello tracks and then fell from a hotel room window. His classic namesake drink, adapted by Sam Ross, is a sinfully sophisticated rum old-fashioned variation. Subtly sweet—unlike Rose's cloying advances—it's as catchy as one of Charlie's jingles. It's best to limit yourself to one or two, though, if you want to avoid getting locked in the dungeon of an unstable admirer.

CHARLIE HARPER

chet baker

2 ounces aged rum
2 bar spoons sweet vermouth
1 bar spoon honey syrup
   (see page 199)

2 dashes of Angostura bitters
2 dashes of orange bitters
1 orange twist, for garnish

Combine the rum, vermouth, honey syrup, and bitters in an old-fashioned glass. Add ice and stir for 5 or 6 seconds. Garnish with the orange twist.

OFGLEN
maid

THE HANDMAID'S TALE

Some heroes choose to wear capes; others are forced to.

Handmaid Ofglen (née Lillie Fuller) was one of hundreds of fertile women in the dystopian Republic of Gilead forced to breed with high-ranking government officials to supply the country's elite with children. Unlike most of her fellow sex slaves, she initially didn't mind having to endure the monthly "ceremonies" with her master, because, as a former homeless junkie, she was just happy to have a place to sleep and food to eat.

All that changed when she refused to participate in the death-by-stoning of a Handmaid convicted of child endangerment, and convinced her colleagues to do the same. As punishment, Ofglen's tongue was ripped out and, with it, any last speck of goodwill she felt toward her captors. Secretly linking up with the Mayday resistance movement, she would get her revenge at the grand opening of the Rachel and Leah Center, where, strapped with explosives, she barged into the christening ceremony like a red-cloaked angel of death, blowing herself up along with dozens of Gilead's top politicians and providing a much-needed jolt of hope to her sisters in bondage.

Coming from a diverse array of backgrounds and lifestyles, the Handmaids were united by the uniquely dire circumstances of their incarceration. Similarly (and much less sinisterly), the Maid, a variation of the East-side Cocktail developed at Milk & Honey in the mid-2000s, features simple, time-honored ingredients that bring out the best in just about any spirit. For those with tongues still intact, this first-class refreshment is perfect for basking in the brief glory of a woman whose shocking bravery single-handedly delivered one of the only triumphant moments on TV's bleakest show.

OFGLEN

maid

2 ounces spirit of choice
1 ounce fresh lime juice
3/4 ounce simple syrup
(see page 200)

5 thin slices cucumber
5 or 6 fresh mint leaves, plus
1 sprig for garnish

Combine the alcohol, lime juice, simple syrup, 3 slices of the cucumber, and the mint leaves in an ice-filled shaker. Shake vigorously and strain into a double old-fashioned glass over ice. Garnish with the remaining 2 slices cucumber and the sprig of fresh mint.

ROBERT FORD
silver fox

WESTWORLD

Who needs to make friends when you can *make* them?

Dr. Robert Ford was the main genius behind Westworld, designing the park's robot hosts and developing their personalities and narrative arcs for decades while serving as the park's creative director. His obsession with his "children"—including robot versions of his dead family members and a secretly created replica of his former business partner, Bernard, who later became a high-ranking park administrator—and his growing distaste for humanity caused friction with his employer, Delos Incorporated, which eventually led to his forced retirement.

But Ford had more than a few tricks left up his sleeve for his bosses. While announcing his last narrative, "Journey into Night," he allowed himself to be fatally shot by Dolores Abernathy, but not before restoring her and several other hosts' memories. The ensuing robot uprising led to the deaths of hundreds of park guests and employees, the destruction of Delos's clandestine DNA-mining operation, and the bloody descent into madness of William, Delos's major shareholder. Having uploaded his consciousness into the digital System that connected all the hosts, "Ford" watched with the satisfaction of a proud parent as his ultimate plan came to fruition: Dolores and

Bernard escaped the park to tackle the challenges of the outside world as fully sentient beings.

Described derisively as a Wizard of Oz–like figure by William, Ford turned out to be far more transcendent than any run-of-the-mill technological trickster. Named for another famously wily creature, the Silver Fox was designed by Dutch Kills Bar's Richard Boccato, and represents a lusciously sweet-and-frothy step in cocktail evolution. This intermingling of orgeat, lemon juice, and egg white is suppler than an Anthony Hopkins soliloquy, and as dangerously easy to consume. On second thought, you might want to enjoy as many of these as you can before the impending robot apocalypse.

ROBERT FORD
silver fox

1 1/2 ounces gin
3/4 ounce fresh lemon juice
1/2 ounce orgeat

1/2 ounce Faretti biscotti liqueur
  or amaretto
1 egg white
Club soda

Combine the gin, lemon juice, orgeat, Faretti, and egg white in a shaker. Shake without ice (to emulsify the egg white) for 10 seconds, then add ice and shake vigorously. Strain into a tall glass filled with ice (preferably one long ice cube, known as a Collins spear). Top with club soda.

DEREK
SHEPHERD

adonis

GREY'S ANATOMY

Dr. Derek Shepherd was arguably TV's most ogled physician since George Clooney's stint on *ER*, and for good reason. The dashing, brilliant, and universally respected chief of surgery at Seattle Grace Hospital regularly performed medical miracles on patients who'd been abandoned by their previous doctors, while passionately romancing his wife and colleague, Dr. Meredith Grey, and taking care of their children, going as far as to treat his adopted daughter Zola's spinal disease.

But it wasn't always smooth sailing for the man known as McDreamy. He started dating Meredith while still married, then left her and went back to his first wife for a brief time. When he finally decided Meredith was the one, he got wasted and nearly destroyed the ring his mother had given him to propose with. Years later, he took a job in Washington, D.C., abandoning Meredith and their young children for a time before deciding to return home. But bad luck (and possibly karma) intervened: after witnessing a car accident and saving the passengers, he was struck by a speeding truck and killed, leaving his family—and *Grey's* fans—with one giant McNightmare.

Despite his obvious shortcomings, Dr. Shepherd is still worshiped as a do-no-wrong, lab-coated Adonis.

The sherry-based cocktail, named for that beautiful, ill-fated Greek god, first appeared on the Waldorf Astoria's menu in 1884 and became a hit with professionals, medical and otherwise, who wanted to enjoy a soothing tipple without the effects of hard liquor. As delicate as McDreamy's hands in the operating room, the Adonis might not be the best pre-surgery beverage, but at least it won't get you sloshed enough to smack your future wife's engagement ring into the woods with a baseball bat.

DEREK SHEPHERD

adonis

1 1/2 ounces fino sherry
1 1/2 ounces sweet vermouth

2 dashes of orange bitters
1 lemon twist, for garnish

Combine the sherry, vermouth, and bitters in a mixing glass filled with cracked ice. Stir with a long-handled spoon for approximately 30 seconds and strain into a stemmed cocktail glass. Garnish with the lemon twist.

BUFFY SUMMERS

summer's day

BUFFY THE VAMPIRE SLAYER

Whether you're roasting supernatural creatures or getting roasted by a biology exam, it's always good to have friends you can count on. Buffy Summers spent her days navigating the teenage drama at Sunnydale High and her nights hunting vampires with her mentor, Giles, and best pals Xander and Willow (aka the Scooby Gang), who always had her back, especially when the undead turned deadly.

In the season 1 finale, Buffy confronted the super-ancient, super-gross-looking vampire known as the Master (ignoring a prophecy that claimed she would die if she tried to fight him), who easily defeated her, sucked her blood, and drowned her in a puddle. On cue, Xander revived her and helped finish off the Master before he could bring his hellish minions to Earth. Years later, when the similarly vicious hell-god, Glory, tried to—duh—open a gateway to Hell, Buffy jumped into the portal, closing it and dying instantly. Willow, assisted by the rest of the gang and an urn from eBay, used a spell to resurrect her BFF and set an almost unbeatable #SquadGoals standard.

Even with its gore-mongering villains and occult plotlines, *Buffy the Vampire Slayer* was, at its core, a mostly lighthearted comedy-drama about kids with unusual extracurricular activities trying to make it relatively unscathed through the awkwardness of ado-lescence. Sharing more than just Buffy's surname, the Summer's Day is a bright and airy take on the gin sour concocted by Milk & Honey's Michael McIlroy, featuring muddled oranges and a satisfyingly frothy finish that evoke Southern California's fresh vibes and bountiful harvests. Described as sunshine in a glass, it's the per-fect tonic for staving off vampires or saluting a young woman whose unrivaled stake-wielding (among other things) stole the hearts of countless '90s teenagers.

BUFFY SUMMERS

summer's day

2 ounces gin
3/4 ounce fresh lemon juice
3/4 ounce simple syrup
(see page 200)

3 thin orange slices
1 egg white
Club soda

Combine the gin, lemon juice, simple syrup, 2 orange slices, and the egg white in a shaker. Shake without ice (to emulsify the egg white) for 10 seconds, then add ice and shake vigorously. Strain into a tall glass filled with ice (preferably one long ice cube, known as a Collins spear). Top with club soda. Garnish with the remaining orange slice.

OZ

It's nearly impossible for anyone to change their stripes, let alone a lifelong uber-racist whose favorite hobbies included sadism and knife-play. Vernon Schillinger was one of the most feared white supremacists at the Oswald State Penitentiary, where he ruled the Aryan Brotherhood and tormented fellow inmate Tobias Beecher, whose brief stint as Schillinger's sex slave turned the formerly meek lawyer into a vicious, revenge-seeking loose cannon.

Schillinger and Beecher's confrontations frequently ended in vicious stabbings and left a grizzly trail of collateral damage, including the lives of Schillinger's two sons and Beecher's son Gary's left hand. Nevertheless, Schillinger continued plotting, raping, and hatemongering until Tobias came to the aid of fellow racist Wilson Loewen, thereby squashing the beef. But all that seemed to end well in Oz never really did, and it wasn't long before Schillinger was accidentally stabbed to death by Beecher during a performance of *Macbeth*, when their mutual lover, the sociopathic Chris Keller, switched out a prop blade for a real one.

At least some of Schillinger's level-10 dickishness can be attributed to his father, who violently ingrained his backward, archaic (yet still sadly prevalent) ideology into his son's already-warped mind. As such, a White Old-Fashioned sounds like something that Schillinger would totally be into (if he drank). But this expertly balanced sipper from Los Angeles's Melrose Umbrella Co. lovingly integrates ingredients from Mexico and South America, cultivated by people whom Schillinger would more likely want to brutalize than toast. Strong enough to erase the visual stench of Schillinger's vile exploits, it's a perfect fuck-you to a man who, unlike many archetypal HBO monsters, got exactly what he deserved.

VERNON SCHILLINGER

white old-fashioned

2 ounces mezcal

1/2 ounce Marie Brizard white crème de cacao

1 bar spoon yellow Chartreuse

2 dashes of orange bitters

1 lemon twist, for garnish

Combine the mezcal, crème de cacao, Chartreuse, and bitters in an old-fashioned glass. Add ice and stir for 5 or 6 seconds. Garnish with the lemon twist.

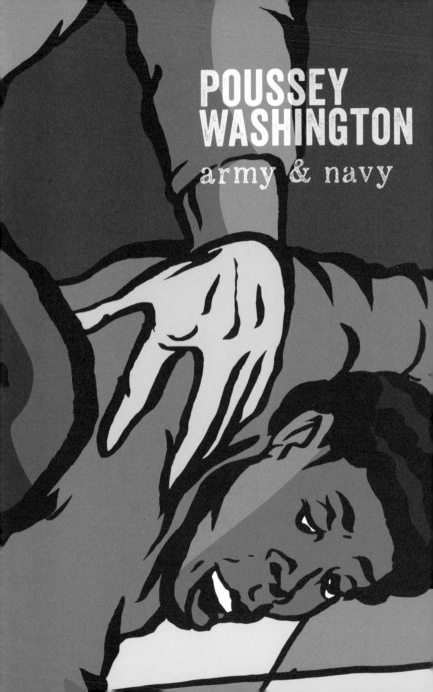

ORANGE IS THE NEW BLACK

Though it's become common knowledge that the TV gods don't discriminate when it comes to snuffing out beloved characters, that doesn't make it sting any less when they do.

Poussey Washington, one of the quirkiest, kindest, and brightest inmates at Litchfield Penitentiary, grew up on various European military bases and fell in love with a German officer's daughter, a doomed romance that set the rebellious, weed-dealing teen on a path to incarceration. At Litchfield, Poussey's unconventional past and easygoing, fair-minded nature made her a favorite of the other prisoners, especially her best friend, Taystee, and lover, Soso. Which is why, when she was accidentally asphyxiated during a protest of the power-hungry guard captain Desi Piscatella (a nod to the real-life 2014 death of Eric Garner), it was all the more gut-twisting for fans and the other inmates, who demanded justice for her in the ensuing prison riot.

Besides her upbeat, silly personality, few things brought as much joy to Litchfield's ladies as a fresh batch of Poussey's incomparable homemade booze. A throwback to an era where befriending a decent hooch-maker was the only way to stay properly pickled, the Army &

Navy recalls Poussey's childhood as a military brat, and has a warm, nutty flavor that's as sweet as her rendition of "Amazing Grace" at the annual prison Christmas pageant. Beefed up with a healthy dollop of Angostura bitters, this criminally smooth treat makes for an ideal pick-me-up when mourning a fascinating woman who brought her unique light to a place in desperate need of it.

POUSSEY WASHINGTON

army & navy

2 ounces gin
3/4 ounce fresh lemon juice

3/4 ounce orgeat
2 dashes of Angostura bitters

Combine the gin, lemon juice, orgeat, and bitters in an ice-filled shaker. Shake vigorously and strain into a stemmed cocktail glass.

BART BASS
chief executive

GOSSIP GIRL

When it came to bad boy Chuck Bass's vengeful, manipulative nature, the apple didn't fall far from the tree. Or, more precisely, from the Upper Manhattan rooftop.

Chuck's father, Bart Bass, the self-made head of Bass Industries, tried to impart his vast (albeit ruthless) business acumen to his son, but mostly ended up alienating him, along with the rest of his socialite Brady Bunch—his second wife, Lily van der Woodsen, and her children—whom he attempted to control by lies, manipulation, and secret private-eye files. After faking his own death to avoid his competitors, Bart was able to reemerge when Chuck helped imprison his father's enemies. Instead of thanking his son, Bart promptly removed Chuck from the company, kick-starting a son-versus-father showdown that uncovered illegal oil deals with Sudan and a failed attempt on Chuck's life. Called out by Chuck for his general dirtbaggery, Bart did what any good sociopathic father would and tried to throw his son off the roof of a building. Karma intervening, Bart stumbled and took the plunge himself, a grotesque end for a truly terrible man.

"I can buy whatever I want," Bart bragged. "It's one of the perks of being really rich." Luckily, you don't need massive, shadily acquired wealth to purchase a drink worthy of TV's slimiest CEO. The Chief Executive, a powerfully smoky and suave sipper from Nashville's Brandon Bramhall, projects a classy confidence that the whiskey-loving Bart would have no choice but to admire. Infused with stomach-settling Gran Classico, it's perfect for cooling off after closing a deal or surviving a confrontation with a vicious boss. And even if you've got penthouse aspirations, just remember that—as with all cocktails—this one's more safely enjoyed on the ground than near a ledge.

BART BASS

chief executive

1 1/2 ounces Islay scotch
1 ounce Gran Classico

1/2 ounce Smith & Cross
    Jamaican rum
1 orange twist, for garnish

Combine the scotch, Gran Classico, and rum in a double old-fashioned glass. Add ice and stir for about 5 seconds. Garnish with the orange twist.

RICHARD
GILMORE

don
lockwood

GILMORE GIRLS

Every family needs someone to hold it together. Luckily for one eccentric Connecticut clan, Richard Gilmore was that person, and then some.

Old-money stickler, for proper etiquette, Richard and his wife, Emily, were appalled when their headstrong, independent daughter, Lorelai, became pregnant at sixteen and left her childhood home, only to return years later when her own daughter, Rory, needed financial help to attend a prestigious prep school. Instead of turning his back, Richard agreed to pay tuition if Rory and Lorelai attended dinner at his home every Friday, a move that, despite the constant friction between his wife and daughter, brought the family closer together. He developed an extraordinarily close bond with Rory (especially after she was accepted to his alma mater, Yale), becoming her greatest fan and protector, a role he played with vigor until his heart gave out shortly before the series was revived in 2016. As devastating as Richard's off-screen departure was, his death forced Emily and Lorelai to seek therapy to work through their issues, something that would certainly have made Papa proud.

Though he eventually accepted his daughter's "scandalous" past, Richard always maintained his traditionalist nature, a bygone sense of decorum exemplified by men like Gene Kelly's character Don Lockwood in *Singin' in the Rain,* whose motto—"Dignity, always dignity"—was a code Richard also tried to live by. The Don Lockwood cocktail, created by Abraham Hawkins at Dutch Kills Bar, is a similarly sophisticated addition to the old-fashioned family. Its no-nonsense yet elegant notes of smoke, bitters, and maple syrup (recalling the Gilmores' New England roots) makes it perfect for a Friday-night toast to that special father/grandfather/husband in your life—or the fictional one you wish you had.

RICHARD GILMORE

don lockwood

1 ounce Islay scotch
1 ounce bourbon
3/8 ounce pure maple syrup

2 dashes of Angostura bitters
2 dashes of chocolate bitters
1 orange twist, for garnish

Combine the scotch, bourbon, maple syrup, and bitters in an old-fashioned glass. Add ice and stir for about 5 seconds. Garnish with the orange twist.

SONS OF ANARCHY

British MP Neil Kinnock famously said, "Loyalty is a fine quality, but in excess it fills political graveyards." When applied to members of biker gangs, the graveyard usually isn't an abstract concept.

Harry "Opie" Winston rose through the ranks of the motorcycle-club-slash-criminal-organization due to his willingness to sacrifice everything for his de facto family and its code, jumping headfirst into lethal confrontations with weapons dealers and rival gangs; refusing to divulge club secrets to his second wife, Lyla; and nearly killing Clay Morrow when he discovered that the crooked Sons of Anarchy president was responsible for the deaths of his first wife and his father. So it was no surprise when Opie voluntarily went to prison to help protect his outnumbered brothers—including his life-long best friend, Jax Teller—from drug kingpin Damon Pope. In one last act of selflessness, he saved Jax's life by nobly taking on four of Pope's lackeys himself, before one savage pipe blow to the head ended it all.

Opie's flawed yet endearing persona made his brutal exit even more agonizing, but he was far from the first "soldier" to fight on in the face of certain annihilation. In 1813, as his ship was being boarded by the British,

Captain James Lawrence shouted a futile order—"Don't give up the ship!"—that became a popular navy rallying cry and the name of an equally bold cocktail first appearing in Crosby Gaige's *Cocktail Guide and Ladies' Companion*. This bright, bitter yet smooth cousin of the martini quietly invades, like the deceptively docile Opie, without any hint of its true potency. But law-abiding imbibers beware: unless you have the leathery liver of a professional outlaw, you may stumble out of bed the morning after feeling like you've been repeatedly bludgeoned with a long piece of metal.

OPIE WINSTON

don't give up the ship

1 1/2 ounces gin
1/2 ounce Fernet-Branca
1/2 ounce sweet vermouth

1/2 ounce orange curaçao
1 orange twist, for garnish

Combine the gin, Fernet, vermouth, and curaçao in a mixing glass filled with cracked ice. Stir for approximately 30 seconds and strain into a stemmed cocktail glass. Garnish with the orange twist.

CONKY
death in the afternoon

TRAILER PARK BOYS

Everyone deals with stress their own way. Thankfully, that doesn't often involve getting bossed around by a deranged puppet. When Bubbles—the bespectacled, shopping-cart-stealing cat-whisperer of Sunnyvale Trailer Park—was in grade school, he used a ventriloquist dummy version of himself named Conky to cope with his problems, until Conky's mischievous, amoral personality began to consume his own, forcing his friends Julian and Ricky to "kill" the creepy toy by tossing him in a swamp.

Years later, Julian fished Conky out to coax Bubbles into seeking treatment for a toothache, but it wasn't long before the puppet was back to his old tricks. He mercilessly taunted Ricky and got the boys caught in a tranquilizer-dart standoff before Julian shot him in the head. Except it still wasn't quite the end. When Bubbles couldn't deal with the pressure of stealing Patrick Swayze's prize-winning toy train, he resurrected an even eviler Conky, who alerted the authorities to Julian and Ricky's international drug-smuggling ring with musician Sebastian Bach and called Bubbles a "googly-eyed bastard," which ultimately broke the spell, allowing him to drown the little shit-apple once and for all.

When drinking to celebrate the death of the darkest part of Bubbles's psyche, one thing's certain: you're going to need a lot of . . . bubbles. The Death in the Afternoon, invented by Ernest Hemingway, is simple—like Bubbles's austere shed-slash-home—yet brutal. A bitter blend of absinthe and Champagne, it's a decadent, sparkling, bitter reminder of the lifestyle Conky gleefully denied Julian and Ricky by foiling several of their get-rich-quick schemes. Hemingway recommended drinking "three to five of these," which sounds excessive, but doesn't come close to the amount of booze and dope the boys needed to forget about Conky's shenanigans.

CONKY

death in the afternoon

1 ounce absinthe   Champagne, chilled

Pour the absinthe into a Champagne flute or stemmed cocktail glass. Top with iced Champagne until sufficiently milky. Sip slowly.

JIMMY DARMODY
french 75

BOARDWALK EMPIRE

For one decorated World War I veteran, the family business turned out to be far deadlier than any battlefield. In 1921, Jimmy Darmody, the illegitimate son of Atlantic City crime boss Commodore Louis Kaestner, returned from Europe to his hometown and began working as a bodyguard for the Commodore's former lieutenant Nucky Thompson, who now controlled most of the city's illicit industries.

Despite his ambition, Jimmy's poor decision-making doomed his criminal career from the start. After being pardoned for bungling a liquor hijacking and nearly starting a war with New York kingpin Arnold Rothstein, he repaid Nucky by plotting to overthrow him and reinstate the Commodore as boss. But it was soon obvious that he was no match for his former mentor. After the torching of his liquor stash; the murder of his wife, Angela; and the loss of his son, Tommy, Jimmy surrendered, completely broken. Nucky showed no remorse for his protégé-turned-rival, shooting him at the foot of Atlantic City's World War I Memorial.

Because of the damage he suffered overseas, Jimmy had one of *Boardwalk*'s most fascinating backstories, which made his relatively quick departure in season 2 an even tougher pill to swallow. A longer-lasting (though fans of Michael Pitt might say "less tasty") product of World War I, the French 75 was named after an artillery weapon with a similar kick. Originally featuring gin as its base spirit, this citrusy crowd-pleaser morphed into a cognac drink when it crossed the Atlantic; unlike the "one boss allowed" American mob mentality, both versions are acceptable and delicious. Just as Nucky was only "half a gangster" until he killed Jimmy, you're only half a cocktail nerd until you've sampled this all-time classic.

JIMMY DARMODY

french 75

1 ounce gin or cognac
1/2 ounce fresh lemon juice
1/2 ounce simple syrup
  (see page 200)

Champagne
1 lemon twist, for garnish

Combine the gin or cognac, lemon juice, and simple syrup in an ice-filled shaker. Shake vigorously and strain into a stemmed cocktail glass or Champagne flute. Top with Champagne. Garnish with the lemon twist.

THE LEFTOVERS

If Kevin Garvey's wacky descents into purgatory taught us anything, it's that you better brush up on your Krav Maga and 1960s folk rock if you want another chance at life.

The years following the October 14 vanishing of 2 percent of the world's population weren't particularly kind to the sleepwalking police chief of Mapleton, New York, who became an unintentional accessory to cult leader Patti Levin's gruesome suicide. Needing an escape, he shipped off with his girlfriend and daughters to the alleged utopia of Jarden, Texas, but was tormented nonstop by Patti's exasperatingly talkative ghost.

Naturally, Kevin sought out a mystic ex-pedophile who fatally poisoned him and sent him to an afterlife resembling a luxury hotel, where he took on the persona of an international assassin and finally rid himself of Patti's spirit. Back on Earth, he was immediately re-murdered by local hothead John Murphy and returned to the hotel, thwarting death again by performing a karaoke version of Simon & Garfunkel's "Homeward Bound." Bewildering at first, Kevin's experiences came in handy later when he heroically rejoined the undead and used his assassin skills to prevent a global apocalypse. Thanks, Kevin!

Because of his intense need to protect those he loved, Kevin was willing to put his faith in several seemingly insane exit strategies. For those looking to take a plunge into the unknown without making the ultimate sacrifice, there are far tastier poisons, like the Act of Faith from Diamond Reef's Dan Greenbaum. While this rum-forward potion might not be as complicated as trying to influence multiple realms of reality, it has enough flavorful nuances to keep the most out-there palate at full attention, and might just be strong enough to help you untangle exactly what the hell happened during *The Leftovers*'s three mind-melting seasons. On second thought, make that a double.

KEVIN GARVEY

act of faith

1 1/2 ounces Jamaican rum
(preferably Appleton Estate
Reserve)
1/2 ounce Cruzan black strap rum
1/2 ounce Pedro Ximénez sherry
1/4 ounce Angostura bitters
1 orange twist, for garnish

Combine the rums, sherry, and bitters in a double old-fashioned glass. Add ice and stir for approximately 5 seconds. Garnish with the orange twist.

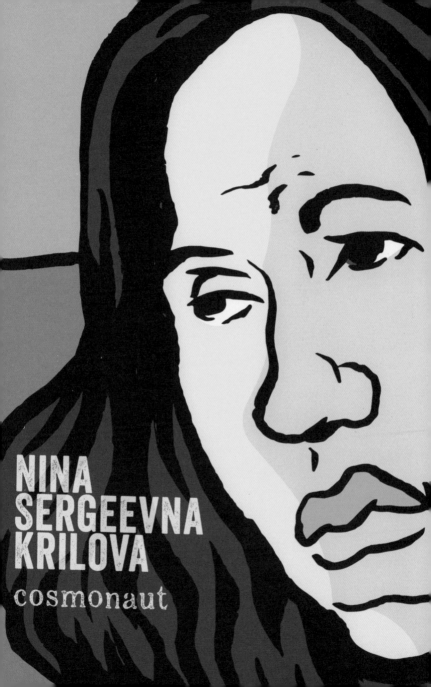

NINA SERGEEVNA KRILOVA

cosmonaut

THE AMERICANS

Think spying for one country is tough? Try being a triple agent. Actually, don't.

Nina Sergeevna Krilova was working undercover for the KGB in the United States, where she was caught by FBI agent—and future lover—Stan Beeman and became his informant. She eventually confessed her treason to her Soviet superiors, who ordered her to keep the fling going to extract information from the Americans, an insanely complicated bit of espionage that led to her helping Directorate S agents Philip and Elizabeth Jennings evade FBI surveillance, but also got her incarcerated in a Soviet prison after she failed to obtain the valuable Echo program from Beeman.

After ruthlessly extracting a confession from another treasonous inmate, Nina was transferred to a secret laboratory where she was ordered to keep tabs on scientist Anton Baklanov, with whom she quickly developed an intimate friendship. Committing a major spy faux pas, she let her emotions get the better of her and was caught trying to help Baklanov smuggle a letter to his son, one last mistake that led to her cold-blooded assassination in the bowels of the gulag, a double victim of love and the Cold War.

Her relationship with Beeman aside, Nina ultimately remained loyal to her homeland, even though the precariousness of her situation often made her feel adrift and alienated from her own people. The Cosmonaut cocktail is a nod not only to Nina's isolation and Soviet roots but also to those of its creator, Sasha Petraske, whose Russian parents imbued him with their ardent love of communism and respect for the laboring classes. This tart, mildly sweet Cosmo upgrade's dollop of jam also provides a healthy dose of Western decadence, bridging the two worlds of a strong, resourceful woman who tragically couldn't survive in either one.

NINA SERGEEVNA KRILOVA

cosmonaut

2 ounces gin
3/4 ounce fresh lemon juice

1 hefty bar spoon of raspberry preserves

Combine the gin, lemon juice, and raspberry preserves in an ice-filled shaker. Shake vigorously and strain into a stemmed cocktail glass.

TASHA YAR
star daisy

STAR TREK: THE NEXT GENERATION

For one intrepid explorer, space really was the final frontier ... twice.

Escaping a violence-filled childhood on the lawless colony planet Turkana IV, Tasha Yar became enamored with Starfleet's mission of universal goodwill. It wasn't long before she was living her best life among the stars as a lieutenant and the chief security officer on the USS *Enterprise-D,* helping to thwart alien nemeses, taking the lead on vital away missions, getting intimate with the android Data, and impressing Lieutenant Worf with her badass martial arts skills—until the end of season 1, when she was randomly killed by a lame slime monster, a death that her fellow crewmembers (and TV critics) viewed as senseless. Luckily, she returned two seasons later in an alternate timeline, where, in a send-off much more befitting her character, she traveled back in time with the *Enterprise-C* to heroically stop an eventual war between the Klingons and the Federation. (She went on to be impregnated and murdered by Romulans, but hey, space happens!)

Most Trekkies were understandably miffed at the show's initial treatment of Tasha, but it would be tough to find anyone in the galaxy to complain about the Star Daisy. Just as reaching the stars has been a human goal since the beginning of time, variations of this refreshingly dry forefather of the sidecar have been served since the first cocktails appeared on bar menus in the early nineteenth century. So whenever you're feeling down about your tactical officer always getting the short end of the futuristic stick, just teleport to your local watering hole for a different kind of subtly strong blond-hued beauty that'll still be sipped long after we conquer warp speed.

TASHA YAR

star daisy

3/4 ounce Laird's Applejack or comparable apple brandy
3/4 ounce gin
3/4 ounce fresh lemon juice
3/4 ounce orange curaçao
2 bar spoons club soda
1 lemon twist, for garnish

Combine the applejack, gin, lemon juice, and curaçao in an ice-filled shaker. Shake vigorously and strain into a stemmed cocktail glass. Top with the club soda. Garnish with the lemon twist.

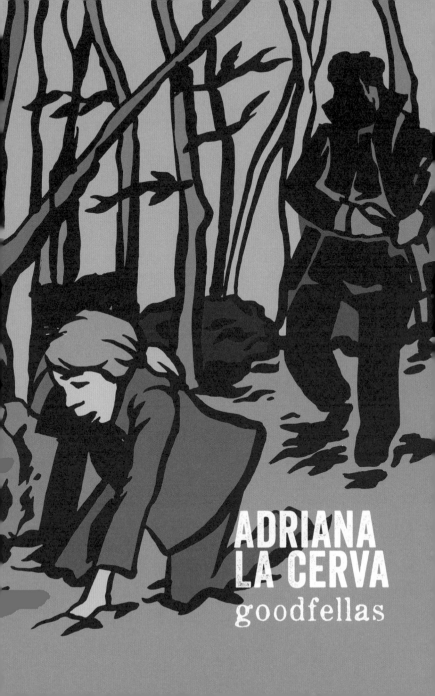

THE SOPRANOS

Anyone willing to give up everything for the chance at a lavish, gangster-movie lifestyle should probably pay attention to how those films usually end. Adriana La Cerva, the niece of some of New Jersey's most notorious mobsters, never had any qualms with the family business, even forgoing a promising career in restaurant management to marry up-and-coming Soprano crew member Christopher Moltisanti.

Despite Christopher's drug use, numerous infidelities, and propensity for domestic violence, Adriana stood by her man, believing that better times were right around the corner once he achieved sobriety and became a Made Man. Nope. While running a nightclub that Christopher "bought" for her, she turned FBI informant after being threatened with prison time for cocaine distribution. The stress was intense enough to give her ulcerative colitis and make her beg her man to join her in witness protection, an offer he politely refused by having his colleague Silvio drive her out to the woods and put a bullet in her skull. Bada bing, bada boom!

A major early supporter of Christopher's failed screenwriting efforts, Adriana ended up with a leading role in the kind of tragedy she wished he'd penned. The Goodfellas, created by Little Branch's Luis Gil and named for that iconic mob flick with an equally volatile romance at its center, is a heavy-hitting blend of scotch and an Italian duo of amaro and vermouth that's as loud as one of Adriana's leopard-print skirts, with a finish as tender as the love she gave to her hard-hearted husband. Perfect for closing a shady deal or dulling the memory of Adriana's ghastly expression when she realized her retirement was going to be far shorter than she'd hoped.

ADRIANA LA CERVA

goodfellas

1 1/2 ounces blended scotch
3/4 ounce Amaro Montenegro

3/4 ounce Carpano Bianco vermouth
1 lemon twist, for garnish

Combine the scotch, amaro, and vermouth in a double old-fashioned glass. Add ice and stir five or six times. Garnish with the lemon twist.

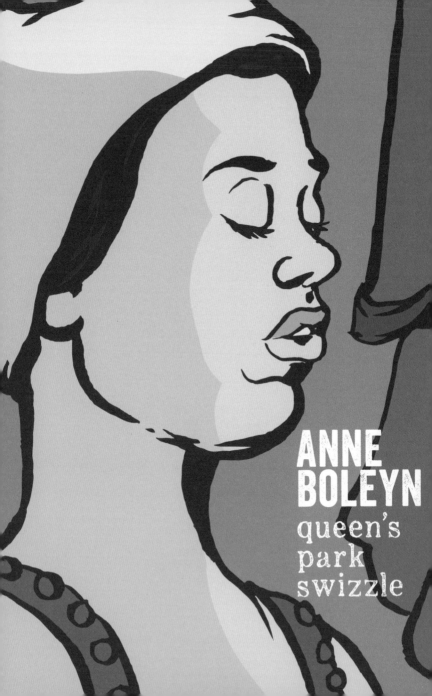

ANNE
BOLEYN

queen's
park
swizzle

THE TUDORS

It's not the best idea to enter a relationship thinking you can fix the other person, but that didn't stop Anne Boleyn. The former lady-in-waiting, armed with uncommon intelligence, the manipulative tactics of her father and uncle, and certain "skills" she picked up in France, started an affair with the already-married Henry VIII, confident she could steal the king's heart, give him the son he desperately desired, and put a permanent end to his womanizing ways. Easy, right?

The plan started out well: Henry had his first marriage annulled, and Anne gave birth to a legitimate heir. Unfortunately for her, that child was a girl, and Henry was soon back to his philandering, no longer impressed with his wife's combative temperament. After she flipped out about Henry's affair with Jane Seymour and miscarried a son, the king and his advisors—who viewed the queen as a barrier to their own political aspirations—had had enough. Falsely accused and convicted of incest, treason, and adultery, she was beheaded outside the Tower of London, where she instantly became history's most famous poster-casualty of absolute monarchs refusing to keep it in their pantaloons.

From the moment she first donned the purple, Anne took full advantage of the respect the monarchy commanded. Among cocktail royalty, few drinks are as admired as the jewel of Trinidad's Queen's Park Hotel, the Queen's Park Swizzle. From its regal crown of bitters and mint to its stylish green-and-white body, it's a beauty to behold, with a bold, fresh personality to match that of Henry's most notable spouse and a mouthfeel as satisfyingly sweet as Anne's daughter, Elizabeth, becoming one of England's most beloved rulers just two decades after her mother's cruel death.

ANNE BOLEYN

queen's park swizzle

2 ounces white rum
1 ounce fresh lime juice
3/4 ounce simple syrup
(see page 200)

6 to 8 fresh mint leaves, plus 1
sprig for garnish
1 brown sugar cube
2 dashes of Angostura bitters
2 dashes of Peychaud's bitters

Muddle the rum, lime juice, simple syrup, mint leaves, and sugar cube in a Collins glass. Fill the glass two-thirds of the way with crushed ice. Add the bitters and stir briefly with a swizzle stick. Fill the glass to the top with crushed ice. Garnish with the mint sprig.

THE WALKING DEAD

The end of the world started out fairly promising for Shane Walsh. Though the Georgia cop was forced to abandon his comatose partner, Rick Grimes, at the onset of the Walker apocalypse, he was able to protect Rick's wife, Lori, and son, Carl, joining a group of survivors camped outside Atlanta. With his combat and firearms skills, pragmatic instincts, and a budding romance with Lori, Shane looked as well positioned as anyone to thrive in post-outbreak America. Until Rick showed up at the camp to reclaim his family and assume leadership of the group. Bummer.

Shane's jealousy toward his former best friend continued to fester during the group's stay at Hershel Greene's farm. Shane became violent and unpredictable, railing against Rick's altruistic impulses, only concerning himself with the survival of Lori, Carl, and Lori's unborn child, which he believed was his. Finally snapping, he lured Rick to a field, where Rick, sensing what was about to happen, shoved a knife into Shane's heart before Carl finished off his reanimated body for good with a bullet.

Unquestionably skilled at taking out walkers, Shane's unhealthy obsession with Lori and feud with Rick ultimately took his focus away from the real enemy, until it was too late. The Zombie, an insidious brainchild of Hollywood's Donn Beach, was turning unsuspecting drinkers into stumbling corpses long before *The Walking Dead* aired. This tiki lover's kryptonite features a deadly blend of three rums (none under 80 proof) and enough tropical vibes to conjure up the paradise Shane failed to find for himself and Rick's family. You probably won't get stabbed by your BFF if you slurrily try to order more than one of these, but you might be asked to take a walk.

SHANE WALSH
zombie

1 1/2 ounces añejo rum

1 1/2 ounces Jamaican rum

1 ounce 151-proof rum

3/4 ounce fresh lime juice

1/4 ounce John D. Taylor's Velvet Falernum

1/4 ounce fresh grapefruit juice

1/4 ounce pomegranate syrup (see page 201)

1/4 ounce cinnamon syrup (see page 200)

1 bar spoon absinthe

Dash of Angostura bitters

1 sprig fresh mint, for garnish

Combine the three rums, lime juice, Falernum, grapefruit juice, pomegranate syrup, cinnamon syrup, absinthe, and bitters in a shaker. Whip (shake without ice) and pour into a tall glass or tiki mug over crushed ice. Garnish with the mint sprig.

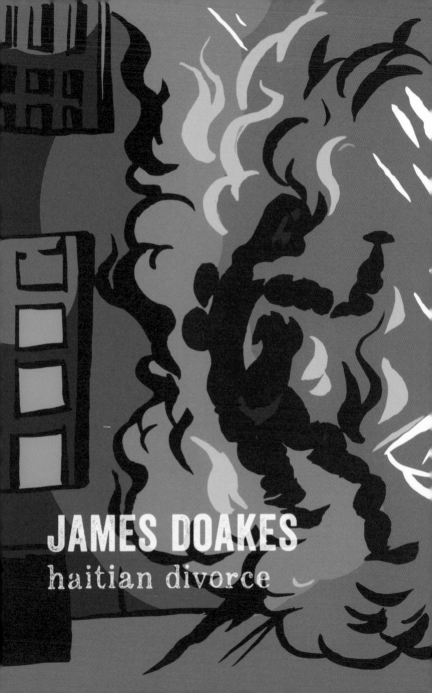

JAMES DOAKES
haitian divorce

DEXTER

It's always fun to theorize that a coworker might be a serial killer, but unless you want to end up like James Doakes, it's best to keep your mouth shut.

The Florida cop cut his teeth as an Army Ranger, fighting Haitian death squads and assassinating high-level special-ops targets before returning home to join the Miami Police Department. His military experience and emotional detachment made him an exemplary member of the Homicide Unit—and an enemy of forensic blood spatter analyst and vigilante serial killer Dexter Morgan. Doakes's suspicions about Dexter's true nature turned into a one-man crusade that ended about as badly as you might expect. He brought incriminating blood samples he found in Dexter's apartment to a friend in Haiti, only to have them intercepted by the FBI, making him the primary suspect in the Bay Harbor Butcher case, and was eventually burned alive in an Everglades cabin by Dexter's psycho ex-girlfriend, Lila Tournay.

Doakes thought that his Haitian connections would help him seal Dexter's fate, but his Haitian sojourn only helped accelerate his own fiery downfall. Tom Richter's Haitian Divorce, named for the once popular practice of couples heading to that country to dissolve their marriages without any legal hassle, is similarly effective for divorcing drinkers from their sobriety. This heavy-hitting, one-two punch of rum and mezcal is stiff enough to warm the heart of even the most stunted barfly, yet it's as carefully balanced as the trigger finger of a trained assassin. While its sedative effects might not rival one of Dexter's syringes, it's still probably not a good option for happy hours with colleagues who might want nothing more than to turn you into fish food.

JAMES DOAKES
haitian divorce

1 1/2 ounces aged rum
3/4 ounce mezcal
1/2 ounce Pedro Ximénez
  sherry

3 dashes of Angostura bitters
1 orange twist, for garnish
1 lime twist, for garnish

Combine the rum, mezcal, sherry, and bitters in an old-fashioned glass. Add ice and stir for 5 or 6 seconds. Garnish with the orange and lime twists.

SALVATORE BONPENSIERO

italian rivalry

THE SOPRANOS

Some snitches get stitches and others disappear into witness protection, but most aren't so lucky. Salvatore "Big Pussy" Bonpensiero spent his early years in northern New Jersey as a celebrated cat burglar (despite notoriously finicky bowels), eventually becoming a respected soldier working under his childhood friend Tony Soprano. A devoted husband and father, he sold heroin on the side to pay his kids' tuition, a move that eventually got him into hot water with the FBI.

Instead of doing his time like any respectable mobster, Pussy decided to become an informant. However, he refused to give the feds any legit info until Tony passed him over for a promotion, after which he sang like a capicola-eating canary to the point that his handler accused him of having Stockholm syndrome. It wasn't long before the always-suspicious Tony found Pussy's wire and invited him on a Fredo Corleone–style fishing trip, sharing one last poignant moment with his former brother over a bottle of hooch before sending Pussy to a watery grave.

Allowing his personal beef with Tony to interfere with a way of life that went back centuries was as good as a death sentence for Pussy. The Italian Rivalry, concocted by Joshua Perez at Middle Branch in 2014, features a robust dose of Amaro Montenegro, an Italian amaro with a tradition to rival the mob's, and a bourbon-and-cognac-based smoothness as unexpected as Pussy stabbing Tony in the back (though with much more cheerful results). Perhaps most important, it makes for a much better final drink than a room-temperature tequila shot below decks on the *Stugots*.

SALVATORE BONPENSIERO

italian rivalry

1 ounce bourbon
1 ounce cognac
1/2 ounce Amaro Montenegro

1 brown sugar cube
1 orange twist, for garnish
1 lemon twist, for garnish

Combine the bourbon, cognac, amaro, and sugar cube in an old-fashioned glass. Muddle the sugar, add ice, and stir for 5 or 6 seconds. Garnish with the orange and lemon twists.

CAMILLA MARKS-WHITEMAN

between the sheets

EMPIRE

When opportunity knocks, start knockin' boots. Though that might not be the most prudent (or even feasible) option for most of us, it almost worked for Camilla Marks—twice.

The conniving English socialite first sunk her claws into Hakeem Lyon, manipulating the much-younger rapper's career (among other things) until his father, Empire Entertainment founder Luscious Lyon, bribed her into leaving his son alone. Not one to fade quietly away, Camilla took her homewrecker game up a notch, waiting until venture capitalist Mimi Whiteman took control of Empire. She then seduced and married the cancer-stricken billionaire, installed herself as chairman, and made Hakeem the CEO, telling him to ditch his new girlfriend, Laura. Instead, the crafty millennial made a sex tape of himself and Camilla and sent it to Mimi. Enraged, Camilla murdered her wife and tried to make it look like an accident, not realizing that she was being filmed by Luscious, who used his incomparable persuasion skills—and a loaded pistol—to convince Camilla to drink the same poison she gave Mimi and restore order to the First Family of Hip-Hop.

The woman whom Cookie Lyon derisively called "Yoko"

was willing to employ any number of cutthroat tactics to get what she wanted, but her skills in the bedroom were her most effective asset. Though its origin, like Camilla's, is somewhat of a mystery, the Between the Sheets gained notoriety during Prohibition for its popularity among "working women" of ill repute. Like any good sidecar riff, this sexy little number has the potential to sneak up and land unassuming imbibers in the most risqué after-hours situations. Which is okay, if you don't mind potentially jeopardizing your life's work over a booty call.

CAMILLA MARKS-WHITEMAN

between the sheets

1 ounce Cointreau
3/4 ounce aged rum
3/4 ounce cognac

1/2 ounce fresh lemon juice
1 lemon twist, for garnish

Combine the Cointreau, rum, cognac, and lemon juice in an ice-filled shaker. Shake vigorously and strain into a stemmed cocktail glass. Garnish with the lemon twist.

MAD MEN

It's no surprise that the most well-to-do professionals have some of the most troubled personal lives, but it can still be a little shocking when those problems are brought to light. London-born Lane Pryce, a mergers-and-acquisitions expert at British advertising agency Puttnam, Powell and Lowe, was sent to Manhattan to manage the finances of the recently acquired Sterling Cooper advertising agency, where he subsequently fired its chief officers in order to start a new firm with them.

Though Lane was a major component of Sterling Cooper Draper Pryce's eventual successes, his personal life was far from prosperous. He temporarily lost his wife and children after succumbing to the liquor-fueled hijinks of his partners, began an affair with a Playboy bunny that ended in a falling-out with his father, and found himself mired in debt despite embezzling thousands of dollars from his company. Caught forging checks by Don Draper, Lane decided to end it all. But he wasn't even that good at suicide, failing to gas himself in his new Jaguar when the car wouldn't start, and finally hung himself from the ceiling of his own office.

Many of Lane's issues stemmed from his inability to acclimate to the sharp cultural differences between New York and his native England. The West End, a recent creation of The Everleigh's Cameron Parish, is meant to evoke the charm and elegance of the London district of the same name. Featuring enough crisp, bitter, and sparkling notes to cheer up the dreariest expat, this low-alcohol sipper is a great alternative for office all-stars who aren't looking to get smashed with the reckless abandon of 1960s advertising executives, or any sad soul in need of a pick-me-up before delving into their personal finances.

LANE PRYCE

west end

1 ounce Cocchi Americano
3/4 ounce Cynar or
   comparable artichoke liqueur

2 dashes of peach bitters
Champagne
1 orange twist, for garnish

Combine the Cocchi Americano, Cynar, and bitters in a double old-fashioned glass. Add ice and stir for about 5 seconds. Top with Champagne. Garnish with the orange twist.

HOMELAND

Everyone has a breaking point, even if it takes becoming a human guinea pig to reach it. Special-ops agent Peter Quinn was best known for his unwavering dedication to the CIA, his enthusiastic—if slightly less than legal—interrogation techniques, and his close friendship with fellow agent Carrie Mathison. After recovering from gunshot wounds suffered during a terrorist ambush at Gettysburg, Peter was sent on treacherous missions to the Middle East and Berlin, where he was captured by ISIS and used as a chemical weapons test subject, leaving him with PTSD and seizure-related memory loss.

Against all odds, Peter made a painful, lengthy recovery and won a subsequent bout with substance abuse. But instead of riding off into the sunset, he returned to the only life he knew, helped uncover a massive government conspiracy, and rode headfirst into a hail of bullets—literally—to save Carrie and president-elect Elizabeth Keane from an assassination plot, accepting the death he'd cheated so many times in a characteristically heroic fashion.

Peter's exit didn't sit well with disgruntled fans, who'd invested so much in his mental and physical trauma for five seasons, only to have it wiped out in one heart-wrenching instant. The Blood & Sand, named for a similarly tragic 1922 film about the rise and senseless downfall of a bullfighter, was first featured in the *Savoy Cocktail Book*. With a moniker that recalls Peter's painful sacrifices, as well as the desert that was home to some of his biggest victories, this unique potation features a robust tang that—much like driving kamikaze-style into a group of well-armed mercenaries—is not for everyone. But for those select few, it's enjoyed with the reckless enthusiasm of a patriot willing to give all for his country.

PETER QUINN

blood & sand

3/4 ounce blended scotch

3/4 ounce sweet vermouth

3/4 ounce Cherry Heering

3/4 ounce fresh orange juice

Combine the scotch, vermouth, Cherry Heering, and orange juice in an ice-filled shaker. Shake vigorously and strain into a stemmed cocktail glass.

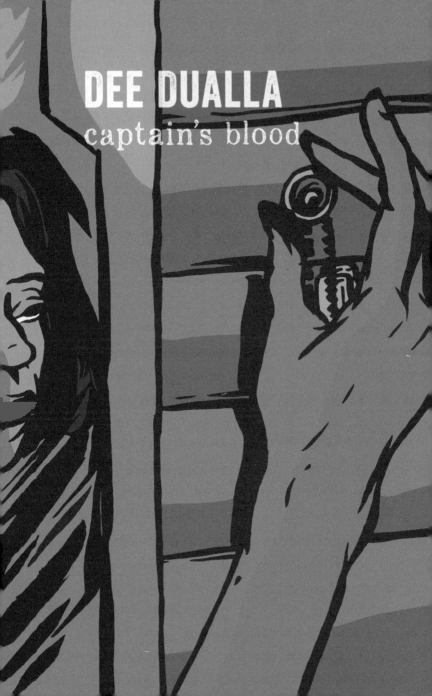

BATTLESTAR GALACTICA

On any long trip, the journey always has the potential to be more fulfilling than the destination. Especially when that destination happens to be an uninhabitable, bombed-out wasteland.

When Anastasia "Dee" Dualla joined the Colonial Fleet against the wishes of her pacifist father, she couldn't have imagined the wild ride fate had planned for her. Escaping the Cylons' obliteration of the Twelve Colonies as a communications officer on the *Galactica*, she expertly handled whatever the job threw at her, coordinating the ship's faster-than-light drives and combat missions and eventually becoming an officer on the *Pegasus* before it was destroyed in the Battle of New Caprica. But it wasn't all business for Dee, who revealed a softer side during her relationship and eventual breakup with Captain Lee Adama. Emotionally overwhelmed when the fleet finally made it to the promised land known as Earth and found it ruined by an ancient nuclear holocaust, she reconciled with Lee and, with military-quick decision-making, blew her brains out, wrongly thinking she had failed the people she'd dedicated her life to protecting.

Never technically commanding her own ship, Dee was just as devoted to the Colonial Fleet—if not more so—as any of its captains. For professional cocktail enthusiasts, few drinks evoke that same level of dedication as the Captain's Blood, a hardy Jamaican-rum daiquiri variation that's been a friend to rugged seafarers (and spacefarers) since it first appeared in Crosby Gaige's 1945 *Cocktail Guide and Ladies' Companion*. A cousin to tiki-style punches, without the frills and garnishes favored by uninitiated civilians, this full-bodied, aromatic tonic is best served as a celebratory relaxer after surviving a long voyage—or for drowning one's sorrows upon discovering that your home was decimated by radiation thousands of years ago.

DEE DUALLA

captain's blood

2 ounces Jamaican rum
1 ounce fresh lime juice
1/2 ounce simple syrup
   (see page 200)

1/4 ounce John D. Taylor's
   Velvet Falernum
4 dashes of Angostura bitters
1 lime wedge, for garnish

Combine the rum, lime juice, simple syrup, Falernum, and bitters in an ice-filled shaker. Shake vigorously and strain into a stemmed cocktail glass. Garnish with the lime wedge.

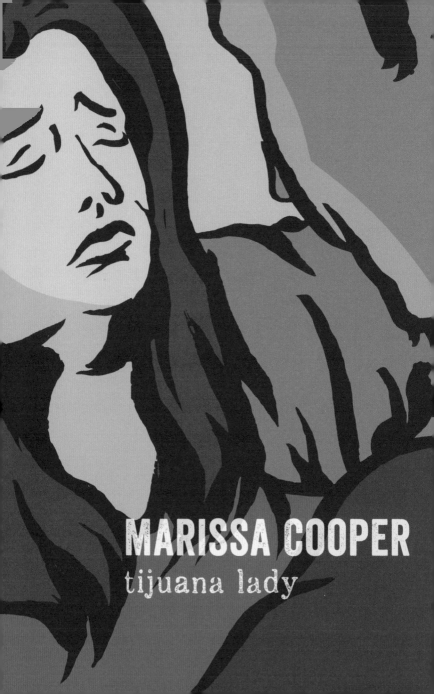

MARISSA COOPER

tijuana lady

THE O.C.

At a casual glance, Harbor School bombshell Marissa Cooper seemed to have it all—stunning looks, a wealthy family, and ride-or-die companions like hotties Ryan Atwood and Summer Roberts. But beneath the glamor lurked a dark and tortured nature, brought on by her parents' messy divorce, her drug abuse, and her horrendous luck with the opposite sex.

Upon learning of her scumbag boyfriend Luke's infidelity while on a trip to Tijuana, Marissa overdosed in an alleyway, where she was saved by Ryan and immediately began dating him. Nobody likes a boring underdog romance, though, so during their many breakups, Marissa's love life was peppered with an increasingly volatile collection of psychos and incompatibles, including Alex Kelly (to get back at her mother for hooking up with Luke—ew), Ryan's rapey brother Trey, and Kevin Volchok, a nutjob she tried to escape by living in Greece for a year. But happiness was never in the cards for the posh princess, who died after Kevin ran her and Ryan off the road on the way to the airport, one last reminder—as if we needed one—that the good life's never all it's cracked up to be.

Marissa's countless questionable decisions, beginning with her breakdown in Mexico, made her a polarizing figure, but it's hard to argue that all that chaos wasn't wildly entertaining. With a moniker alluding to that fateful vacation, Michael Madrusan's Tijuana Lady is a slightly sweet margarita riff with an icily svelte exterior and a surprising underlying complexity. Its citrus, vanilla, and herbal components mingle as smoothly as the cool kids after school, and might have you—like Marissa to Ryan—coming back for seconds (and thirds). Just make sure to get your drinking in before last call, because outside of teenage soap operas, no one likes a drama queen.

MARISSA COOPER
tijuana lady

1 1/2 ounces reposado tequila
1 ounce Licor 43
3/4 ounce fresh lime juice

2 dashes of Angostura bitters
1 lime wedge, for garnish

Combine the tequila, Licor 43, lime juice, and bitters in an ice-filled shaker. Shake vigorously and strain into a stemmed cocktail glass. Garnish with the lime wedge.

DOWNTON ABBEY

Though it's famously been sung that you can't hurry love, things would have probably been a lot better for Matthew Crawley if he hadn't waited.

When the dashing London solicitor became heir to the Earldom of Grantham, he was invited by the family's patriarch, Lord Robert, to live at Downton Abbey, where he quickly fell head over heels for Robert's somewhat haughty daughter Mary. Sharing an ardent kiss with him after consuming a timeless aphrodisiac (sandwiches!), Mary accepted Matthew's proposal, only to back out over questions about his middle-class background. Instead of fighting for love, he joined the army and got engaged to Lavinia Swire, who conveniently died of Spanish influenza just as Mary decided she wanted to get back with her one true boo. After dealing with his guilt over Lavinia's death, Matthew beat up Mary's new fiancé and finally became the model husband he was meant to be—which made watching him die in a car accident while racing home to announce the birth of his and Mary's son a year later all the more horrific.

Matthew's loyal spirit endeared him not only to Lord Robert but also to his other would-be father-in-law, Reginald Swire, whose fortune Matthew inherited and used to save the abbey. The Son-in-Law, a toned-down version of the Mother-in-Law (from Ted Haigh's *Vintage Spirits and Forgotten Cocktails)*, is a bourbon-heavy blend with a regal mouthfeel worthy of the most respected relative-by-marriage (and relative) in Downton. Though its first sip might be a bit astringent, like Mary's initial reaction to Matthew, the drink also features floral notes, and an herbal, citrusy finish that evokes the depth—and tragically fleeting nature—of their marriage. Luckily for whiskey hounds, you won't have to survive a war for a second helping of this liquid love.

MATTHEW CRAWLEY

son-in-law

1 1/2 ounces bourbon
1/2 ounce maraschino liqueur
1/2 ounce orange curaçao
1/2 ounce Amer Picon or
   Amaro CioCiaro

2 dashes of Angostura bitters
2 dashes of Peychaud's bitters
1 brandied cherry, for garnish

Combine the bourbon, maraschino, curaçao, Amer Picon, and bitters in a mixing glass filled with cracked ice. Stir with a long-handled spoon for approximately 30 seconds and strain into a stemmed cocktail glass. Garnish with the brandied cherry.

HERSHEL GREENE
dr. henderson

THE WALKING DEAD

If you're planning on surviving a zombie apocalypse, you're going to want someone like Hershel Greene on your side. The veterinarian-slash-farmer was wary (i.e., kind of a racist douche) about letting Rick Grimes's group stay on his property while patching up Rick's son's injuries from a hunting accident. But after facing a Walker stampede, Hershel came to grips with reality and became an invaluable member of the community Rick established at the West Georgia Correctional Facility. Despite having been bitten by a Walker and losing a leg as a result, Hershel saved dozens of lives, and fearlessly put down the ones he couldn't.

Medical skills aside, Hershel was a trusted advisor, a loving father, and a positive influence on almost everyone he encountered. Except for psychopaths like Philip "The Governor" Blake, who kidnapped Hershel during his second attempt to infiltrate the prison, ignoring the much-wiser man's pleas for peace. In a world where arguments were settled by murders instead of Twitter rants, Hershel didn't stand a chance. He was beheaded by the Governor, zombified, and snuffed out by his friend Michonne, a messy, drawn-out execution that, even for desensitized DeadHeads, was especially nightmare-inducing.

From saving Carl's life with scavenged supplies to temporarily easing the prison's flu epidemic with foraged plants, Hershel was an expert at making the most of what he had. Originally introduced by Fergus Henderson at his London restaurant St. John and credited to his physician father, the Dr. Henderson is a minty hangover remedy for those lacking fancy pills and IV drips. Featuring Fernet-Branca and crème de menthe, it's been described as "toothpaste for the liver," which sounds only slightly better than the anesthesia-free surgeries Hershel performed, but still makes a much better alternative for ending morning-after misery than a katana through the skull.

HERSHEL GREENE

dr. henderson

1 ounce Fernet-Branca   1 ounce crème de menthe

Combine the fernet and crème de menthe in an old-fashioned glass. Add ice and stir for 5 or 6 seconds.

WALTER WHITE
penicillin

BREAKING BAD

High school chemistry teacher to ruthless drug king-pin isn't usually the most advisable career path, but it certainly paid off for the man known on the streets as Heisenberg. Diagnosed with stage IIIA lung cancer on his fiftieth birthday, mild-mannered Walter White made the drastic decision to start producing meth-amphetamine to support his family. Alongside his un-trusty sidekick, Jesse Pinkman, he became one of the most sought-after manufacturers in Albuquerque and a feared figure in that city's underworld.

During Walt's epic transformation from meek to mur-derous, he killed off most of his competitors, obsessively tweaked his production methods, and amassed $80 million, all while his disease went into remission. But life wasn't all meth-flavored gravy. His insatiable hubris led to the destruction of his marriage, the loss of most of his for-tune, and a well-deserved breakup with Jesse, who sold him out to the DEA. Utterly abandoned, Walt made one last-ditch effort to set things right, establishing a trust fund for his children and rescuing Jesse from the Aryan Brotherhood in a blaze of machine-gun-enhanced glory, a surprisingly tidy ending for a man who took the term "dirty money" to another level.

"I'm in the empire business," the seldom-humble

Walt once told Jesse, an empire that would never have existed without his genius-level science background. Sam Ross's ubiquitous Penicillin, named after twentieth-century chemistry's most important breakthrough, has been as integral to contemporary cocktail culture as Walter's product was to discerning drug fiends. Fortified by both blended and single-malt scotch—Walt's poison of choice—this citrusy, ginger-laced revelation has inspired numerous riffs and reinterpretations and established a ravenous cult following. But like Heisenberg's notorious Blue Sky, it's tough to beat the original—a monument of twenty-first-century mixology that will be talked about as long as one of TV's all-time antiheroes will.

WALTER WHITE

penicillin

2 ounces blended scotch
3/4 ounce fresh lemon juice
3/8 ounce honey syrup
(see page 199)

3/8 ounce ginger syrup
(see page 199)
1/4 ounce Islay scotch
1 piece candied ginger, for garnish

Combine the blended scotch, lemon juice, honey syrup, and ginger syrup in an ice-filled shaker. Shake vigorously and strain into a double old-fashioned glass over ice. Float the Islay scotch. Garnish with the candied ginger.

NATHANIEL FISHER SR.

the business

SIX FEET UNDER

It makes sense, almost too obviously, that a show about undertakers would have a notable death scene in its pilot. But randomly killing a hugely important character in the first five minutes? That was a game-changer, for both TV and the First Family of Funerals.

When Nathaniel Fisher Sr., the chain-smoking proprietor of Fisher & Sons Funeral Home, was killed in a traffic accident, it brought the surviving Fishers closer to their deceased patriarch than ever before, literally. Sporting his work suit and trademark gallows humor, he frequently appeared postmortem in visitations that were far more fruitful than freaky: advising his sons, Nate and David, on how to preserve his life's work; helping David accept his homosexuality; consoling his daughter, Claire, while mocking his own funeral; and releasing his wife, Ruth, from the guilt she felt over an affair. And honestly, who wouldn't want to hang out with their dad while he's sipping a cocktail and throwing shade at his own burial?

Whether he was a ghostly apparition or, according to buzzkill showrunner Alan Ball, a manifestation of *Six Feet Under*'s living characters' internal dialogues, Nathaniel was as integral to the future of his family's business as he was to its past. The Business, a dryer, tarter version of the classic Bee's Knees, was first adapted by the late, great Sasha Petraske, a man as synonymous with modern cocktail culture as Fisher & Sons was to the fictional death care industry. Simple and straightforward, like Nathaniel's approach to the funeral business, this lethally drinkable life-enhancer has more soothing properties than the calming voice of an attentive undertaker, with enough underlying sweetness to make even the most corpselike curmudgeon thankful for another day above ground.

NATHANIEL FISHER SR.

the business

2 ounces gin
1 ounce fresh lime juice

3/4 ounce honey syrup
(see page 199)
1 lime wedge, for garnish

Combine the gin, lime juice, and honey syrup in an ice-filled shaker. Shake vigorously and strain into a stemmed cocktail glass. Garnish with the lime wedge.

JOHN LOCKE
island old-fashioned

LOST

Getting stranded on a malevolently supernatural land-mass seems like it would be the start of a very bad time, but not for John Locke. The former foster child's life was fraught with constant trauma, heartbreak, and eventually paralysis, but he remained mostly upbeat despite his dis-ability. His positivity was seemingly rewarded when he not only survived the crash of Oceanic Flight 815 but also regained the use of his legs upon mounting the Island.

This miracle sparked a desire in Locke to protect his new home by any means—including, you know, murder—so it wasn't long before he was considered persona non grata by most of 815's survivors. After learning about the sordid history of the DHARMA Initiative, and despite his poor people skills, he decided to insert himself as leader of the Others. Not surprisingly, he failed to stop the Is-land from dangerously flashing through time, and was eventually strangled by the Others' previous leader, Ben Linus. But because *Lost* worked in mysterious and mostly insane ways, he was able to make amends with those he'd wronged in an alternate post-death timeline, a radical nar-rative shift that irked fans but gave Locke some of the clo-sure he desperately needed.

His unwavering belief in himself and the Island didn't sit well with the less spiritually inclined, like rival Jack

Shephard, but Locke's faith unquestionably helped him survive longer than most in an impossibly hostile environment. Featuring comforting notes of almond and cane syrup, the Island Old-Fashioned, a miracle of friendlier archipelagos crafted by Joseph Schwartz at Little Branch, conjures the Island's healing properties without any of its less-savory aspects. Able to convert whiskey fiends into rum lovers with an ease that Locke never achieved while trying to recruit adherents to his cause, it's strong and smooth enough to sort out the flashback, flash-forward, and flash-sideways pandemonium that made *Lost* one the most addictive yet frustrating shows of all time.

JOHN LOCKE

island old-fashioned

2 ounces aged rum
1 bar spoon John D. Taylor's
  Velvet Falernum

1 bar spoon cane syrup
2 dashes of Angostura bitters
1 orange twist, for garnish

Combine the rum, Falernum, cane syrup, and bitters in an old-fashioned glass. Add ice and stir for about 5 seconds. Garnish with the orange twist.

MR. ROBOT

On a show where almost nothing was as it seemed, Joanna Wellick's motivations were refreshingly straightforward: helping her yuppie spouse, Tyrell, rise to E Corp's upper echelon by any means necessary and getting tied down for the occasional BDSM session, despite her late-term pregnancy.

After Tyrell lost out on a coveted promotion to Scott Knowles; murdered Scott's wife, Sharon; disappeared; and was publicly blamed for the society-leveling Five/Nine hack, Joanna was still determined to clear her husband's name. She goaded Scott into beating her and seduced a bartender named Derek, whom she used to frame Scott for his wife's death. But in her relentless quest to keep up appearances, she forgot about the little guy. Derek (who saw himself as more than just another bondage buddy) shot Joanna after she pledged her love for Tyrell on TV, and just like that, a woman cunning enough to outwit the FBI by inducing her own labor with a serving fork was done in by a simple drink-slinger's broken heart.

Joanna seemed primed for a major role in the ongoing war between Tyrell and E Corp, until her seductive abilities came back to bite her, and not in the way she preferred. While the term might not do full justice to her outrageous bedroom antics, the Hanky Panky is anything but bland. This sexy number, created by Ada Coleman—a woman known as much for her bar skills as her wealthy benefactors—ups the ante with a sultry shock of fernet and a double dose of vermouth that's vital for keeping a clear head during a corporate take-over, or cooling off after reliving the steamy exploits of a power-hungry femme fatale who met her fate much sooner than expected.

JOANNA WELLICK

hanky panky

1 1/2 ounces gin
1 1/2 ounces sweet vermouth

1/4 ounce Fernet-Branca
1 orange twist, for garnish

Combine the gin, vermouth, and fernet in a mixing glass filled with cracked ice. Stir for approximately 30 seconds and strain into a stemmed cocktail glass. Garnish with the orange twist.

MOIRA QUEEN
troublemaker

ARROW

When the karma from your poor decisions comes back to reckon with you—as it always does—just hope that it doesn't take the form of a vengeful mercenary with a sword.

Moira Queen spent years cultivating a positive reputation as the CEO of Queen Consolidated and a Starling City mayoral candidate. But her relationship with her children, Oliver and Thea, was far from sparkling, especially when Oliver returned from Lian Yu as the vigilante archer Green Arrow. When the secrets she'd kept from them—that she'd forced a woman Oliver impregnated to disappear, that Thea was the product of an affair with rival CEO Malcolm Merlyn, that she'd helped Merlyn to destroy the Glades—came to light, they ruined both her family and her shot at the mayor's office. To make amends for her general crappiness, she let Slade Wilson stab her in the gut, trading her children's lives for her own. Which was nice, but it still wasn't like anyone was going to play "Dear Mama" at her funeral.

"You never stop to think what you might do to them," Moira said, referring to the troublesome effect that her lies and manipulations had on those she loved, a dark cloud that still lingered after she sacrificed her life. Danny Gil's Troublemaker is an invigorating take on a Pimm's

Cup that's as satisfying as a perfect bull's-eye, and as well dressed and balanced as Moira appeared in her public life, without all the underlying drama the drink's name implies. The next time you find yourself in a family feud, recuperate with one of these, and be thankful that your mother isn't an amoral adulteress who misleads you about your identity and is partially responsible for murdering hundreds of innocents. And if she is, have another round . . . or five.

MOIRA QUEEN

troublemaker

1 ounce pisco
1 ounce sweet vermouth
3/4 ounce fresh lemon juice
1/2 ounce simple syrup
  (see page 200)

5 thin cucumber slices
3 halved strawberries, plus 1
  whole strawberry for garnish
Club soda

Combine the pisco, vermouth, lemon juice, simple syrup, 3 cucumber slices, and the halved strawberries in an ice-filled shaker. Shake vigorously and strain into a tall glass filled with ice (preferably one long ice cube, known as a Collins spear). Top with club soda. Garnish with the remaining cucumbers slices and the whole strawberry.

TERI BAUER

after all

24

Whenever you think you've had the worst day ever, do yourself a favor and revisit Teri Bauer's last 24 hours.

When Teri's bratty daughter, Kim, disappeared shortly after midnight, Teri went off to find the teen with a man she thought was Kim's friend's father, a terrorist named Kevin who was part of a group trying to force Teri's husband, Jack Bauer, to assist in the assassination of a senator. Catching on to Kevin's kidnap-y vibes, Teri ran away, only to be captured and brought to a warehouse where she was sexually assaulted before shooting her rapist and escaping in a helicopter. Later, while hiding in a "safe" house, she discovered she was pregnant, was attacked by more terrorists, and suffered amnesia after thinking Kim died in a car crash. Escaping once more, Teri returned to the Counter Terrorism Unit, where, as punishment for discovering that Agent Nina Myers was a mole, she was shot in the gut and bled out in her husband's arms just as the clock struck midnight again. And you still want to complain about your crappy commute?

After everything Teri went through during her one-day ride on the 24 roller coaster, watching her helpless death made for one of the most difficult to stomach (pun intended) moments on a show that elevated cruelty to an art form. For those who have faced seemingly impossible odds but lived to trudge through another day, there's the After All, which first appeared in Harry MacElhone's *Cocktails and Barflies*. Fruity yet dry, boozy yet easy-sipping, it's a powerful reminder of the woman whose death gave Jack the motivation to become the full-blown torture-loving maniac we know and love, and perfect for giving yourself a little blissful amnesia, minus the family-related trauma.

TERI BAUER

after all

1 1/2 ounces Laird's Applejack or comparable apple brandy
1 ounce peach liqueur

1/2 ounce fresh lemon juice
1 lemon twist, for garnish

Combine the applejack, peach liqueur, and lemon juice in an ice-filled shaker. Shake vigorously and strain into a stemmed cocktail glass. Garnish with the lemon twist.

SYRUPS

ginger
syrup

To make ginger juice, simply grate peeled fresh ginger and squeeze the pulp between your fingers to release the juice.

1 part superfine sugar
1 part fresh ginger juice

Combine the sugar and ginger juice in a nonreactive container and stir until the sugar has completely dissolved. Cover and refrigerate for up to 5 days.

honey
syrup

3 parts honey
1 part hot water

Combine the honey and hot water in a container and stir until well blended. Cover and refrigerate for up to 5 days.

simple syrup

1 part superfine sugar
1 part water

Combine the sugar and water in a container and stir until the sugar has dissolved. Do not boil. Cover and refrigerate for up to 5 days.

cinnamon syrup

1 cup superfine sugar
1 cup water
3 cinnamon sticks, crushed

Combine the sugar, water, and cinnamon in a medium saucepan and bring to a boil over medium heat, stirring until the sugar has completely dissolved. Simmer for 2 minutes, then remove from the heat. Strain into a glass storage container. Cover and refrigerate for up to 5 days.

pomegranate
syrup

A tangy alternative to grenadine.

1 cup (8 ounces) pomegranate juice concentrate (such as
  FruitFast)
4 cups simple syrup

Combine the pomegranate juice concentrate and simple syrup
in a container and stir until well blended. Cover and refrigerate
for up to 5 days.

ACKNOWLEDGMENTS

Much thanks and gratitude to the many people who made this book possible.

First, to my agent, Rica Allannic, for your amazing insight and encouragement from day one.

To the inimitable Emma Brodie and the rest of the Morrow crew—Liate Stehlik, Cassie Jones, Benjamin Steinberg, Susan Kosko, Andrew DiCecco, Dale Rohrbaugh, Bonni Leon-Berman, Mumtaz Mustafa, Yeon Kim, Gena Lanzi, and Kate Hudkins—for making this the most fun, seamless, and satisfying project from start to finish.

To illustrator extraordinaire Keni Thomas—I couldn't imagine anyone else's ink on these pages.

To the incredible bartenders, both living and gone, whose work has enriched this book, thanks for letting me spread the love.

To the late Sasha Petraske and the rest of the Little Branch family, especially Luis Gil, Lauren Schell, Ben Schwartz, Jen Schwartz, Becky McFalls-Schwartz, Vito Dieterle, Lucinda Sterling, Travis Hernandez, and Michael Timmons, for infinitely expanding my PBR-and-a-shot palate and teaching me more than I ever thought possible. It's been a hell of a decade.

And last, to my parents, for their unflinching support (and Netflix and HBO passwords); my roommates, Sean and Tomas, for putting up with the endless binge-watching; and the countless friends and barflies who offered tips (both practical and monetary) along the way.

my own dearly departed list

ABOUT THE AUTHOR

CHRIS VOLA is the author of two novels and a collection of stories. A graduate of the Columbia University MFA Writing Program, he lives in Manhattan and bartends at the West Village speakeasy Little Branch, where he trained under cocktail legend Sasha Petraske. This is his first book about cocktails and television

HarperCollins books may be purchased for educational, business, or sales promotional use. For information, please e-mail the Special Markets Department at SPsales@harpercollins.com.

FIRST EDITION

Designed by Bonni Leon-Berman

Illustrations copyright © 2019 by Keni Thomas

Library of Congress Cataloging-in-Publication Data has been applied for.

ISBN 978-0-06-288712-2

19 20 21 22 23   SC   10 9 8 7 6 5 4 3 2 1